What Is Intelligence?

Over the past century there have been massive increases in IQ test scores. Many psychologists have struggled to understand the implications of these IQ gains. Do they mean that each generation is more intelligent than the last? Do they suggest how each of us can enhance our own intelligence? These gains were called the "Flynn effect" to recognize the central role played by James R. Flynn in measuring them. However, Flynn himself confessed that he was unsure of their significance.

Finally, in *What is Intelligence? Beyond the Flynn Effect*, Professor Flynn is ready to take a stand. One of the most creative and influential psychologists working in the field of intelligence, he offers a new picture of human intelligence that is both surprising and illuminating.

What is Intelligence? bridges the gulf that separates our minds from those of our ancestors a century ago. It is a fascinating book that makes an important – and lasting – contribution to our understanding of the evolution of human intelligence.

JAMES R. FLYNN is Professor Emeritus at the University of Otago, New Zealand, and a recipient of the University's Gold Medal for Distinguished Career Research. In 2007, the International Society for Intelligence Research named him its Distinguished Scientist of the Year.

What Is Intelligence?

Beyond the Flynn Effect

JAMES R. FLYNN

CAMBRIDGE
UNIVERSITY PRESS

CAMBRIDGE UNIVERSITY PRESS
Cambridge, New York, Melbourne, Madrid,
Cape Town, Singapore, São Paulo

Cambridge University Press
The Edinburgh Building, Cambridge CB2 8RU, UK

Published in the United States of America by
Cambridge University Press, New York

www.cambridge.org
Information on this title: www.cambridge.org/9780521880077

First published 2007

Printed in the United States of America

A catalogue record for this book is available from the British Library

Library of Congress Cataloguing in Publication data

Flynn, James Robert, 1934–
  What is intelligence? Beyond the Flynn effect / James R. Flynn.
    p.   cm.
  Includes bibliographical references and indexes.
  ISBN-13: 978-0-521-88007-7 (hardback : alk. paper)
  ISBN-10: 0-521-88007-6 (hardback : alk. paper)
1. Intellect.   I. Title.

  BF431.F57 2007
  153.9–dc22   2007012361

ISBN 978-0-521-88007-7 hardback

To Bill Dickens

Whose intelligence solved the fourth paradox

The Flynn Effect is important . . . it is such novel facts, when fully investigated, that lead to an increased level of understanding. (Arthur Jensen, *The g factor: The science of mental ability*, p. 330)

What he knew, and what they could not have known, was that their species would change and that he, a modern man, . . . was not quite human in the same way as they had been. (Sebastian Faulks, *Human traces*, p. 205)

Contents

Figures

Tables

Boxes

Acknowledgments

Thanks to John Rust who saw merit in a paper on which this book is based and offered to take it to Cambridge University Press. The scholars whose work has inspired me are cited throughout and some have been singled out in Box 8 in the text.

Publishers have been generous in allowing me to adapt material from several articles. I thank the American Psychological Association for permission to use and adapt material from: J. R. Flynn, "The hidden history of IQ and special education: Can the problems be solved?", *Psychology, Public Policy, and Law* 6 (2000): 191–198; and J. R. Flynn, "Tethering the elephant: Capital cases, IQ, and the Flynn effect," *Psychology, Public Policy, and Law*, 12 (2006): 170–178. I thank Lawrence Erlbaum Associates for the same courtesy for J. R. Flynn & L. G. Weiss, "American IQ gains from 1932 to 2002: The WISC subtests and educational progress," *International Journal of Testing*, 7 (2007): 1–16. Tables 3 and 4 are based on these sources.

I thank ArtMed Publishers of Porto Alegre, Brazil, for permission to use and adapt material from J. R. Flynn, "Efeito Flynn: Repensando a inteligência e seus efeitos" [The Flynn effect: Rethinking intelligence and what affects it], in C. Flores-Mendoza & R. Colom (eds.), *Introdução à psicologia das diferenças individuais* [Introduction to the psychology of individual differences] (2006), pp. 387–411. Tables 1 and 5 are based on this source. Finally, I thank Erlbaum once again for material from J. R. Flynn, *Asian Americans: Achievement beyond IQ* (1991).

1 A bombshell in a letter box

> The special function of scientific explanation is ... to turn the
> unexpected, as far as possible, into the expected.
> (Stephen Toulmin, *Reason in ethics*, p. 88)

I am a teacher and rarely write for specialists alone. I have tried to
avoid the dead-stick prose so beloved by journal editors. Anyone
with a good education or a major in psychology should be able to
read this book and the former is more important than the latter. It
assumes that everyone is interested in intelligence and would like
something exciting to provide a reason to learn more about it.
Specialists will find that much has been omitted but will also,
I hope, find something new in the argument and something
worth pursuing in the research designs recommended.

A warning for everyone: there are problems that can simply
be settled by evidence, for example, whether some swans are black.
But there are deeper problems that pose paradoxes. Sometimes the
evidence that would solve them lies in an inaccessible past. That
means we have to retreat from the scientific level of explanation to
the historical level where we demand only a plausibility that con-
forms to the known facts. I believe that my efforts to resolve the
historical paradoxes we will discuss should be judged by whether
someone has a more satisfactory resolution to offer. The reader
should be wary throughout to distinguish the contentions I evidence from the contentions to which I lend only plausibility.

"The Flynn effect" is the name that has become attached to
an exciting development, namely, that the twentieth century saw

massive IQ gains from one generation to another. To forestall a diagnosis of megalomania, the label was coined by Herrnstein and Murray, the authors of *The bell curve*, and not by myself. I have never done any studies of IQ trends over time in the sense of actually administering tests. Of those who had measured IQ gains here or there, Reed Tuddenham was the first to present convincing evidence using nationwide samples: he compared the mental test scores of US soldiers in World Wars I and II and found huge gains. Had I thought of attaching a name to the phenomenon, I would have offered his.

About 1981, it struck me that if IQ gains over time had occurred anywhere, they might have occurred everywhere and that a phenomenon of great significance was being overlooked. Therefore, I began a survey to see what data existed throughout the developed world. It was on a rather dull Saturday in November 1984 that I found a bombshell in my letter box.

It was data from the distinguished Dutch psychologist P. A. Vroon and some things were evident at a glance. Although Vroon had not developed the techniques to measure them, young Dutch males had made enormous gains in a single generation on an IQ test of forty items selected from Raven's Progressive Matrices. The sample was exhaustive. Raven's was supposed to be the exemplar of a culturally reduced test, one that should have shown no gains over time as culture evolved. These 18-years olds had reached the age at which performance on Raven's peaks. Therefore, their gains could not be dismissed as early maturation, that is, it was not just a matter that children today were about two years ahead of the children of yesterday. Current people would have a much higher IQ than the last generation even after both had reached maturity.

Over a period of twelve months, I was bombarded with data from another thirteen nations all of which showed huge gains. Today the total is almost thirty and includes data from developing nations as well. Our advantage over our ancestors is relatively uniform at all ages from the cradle to the grave. Whether these gains will persist into the twenty-first century is problematic, at least for developed nations. But there is no doubt that they dominated the twentieth century and that their existence and size were quite unexpected. The very fact they occurred creates a crisis of confidence: how could such huge gains be intelligence gains? Either the children of today were far brighter than their parents or, at least in some circumstances, IQ tests were not good measures of intelligence. Paradoxes started to multiply. Now read on.

2   Beyond the Flynn effect

> Yesterday upon the stair
> I saw a man who wasn't there
> He wasn't there again today
> How I wish that man would go away
> > (Nursery rhyme)

I will try to make the problems posed by IQ gains go away, but do not really think that I can say the final word. I claim only that I can at last propose an interpretation that eliminates paradoxes. These paradoxes have been so intimidating as to freeze our thinking about the significance of IQ gains ever since we began to take them seriously (Flynn, 2006a).

Intelligence and the atom

Before I state the paradoxes, there are some concepts to convey. My fundamental line of argument will be that understanding intelligence is like understanding the atom: we have to know not only what holds its components together but also what splits them apart. What binds the components of intelligence together is the general intelligence factor or g; what acts as the atom smasher is the Flynn effect or massive IQ gains over time; the best IQ test to exemplify both of these is called the WISC (Wechsler Intelligence Scale for Children).

The WISC has ten subtests that measure various cognitive skills. For example, the Similarities subtest measures the ability to perceive what things have in common; the Vocabulary subtest measures whether you have accumulated a large number of the words used in everyday life; Information measures your store of general (as distinct from specialized) information; Arithmetic measures your ability to solve everyday mathematical problems (how much change you should have if you bought certain items out of a five-dollar bill); and so forth (see Box 1).

Box 1

The WISC IQ test (The Wechsler Intelligence Scale for Children) has been administered since 1950 to children ages 6 to 16. The ten subtests given throughout most of that period are below (all items used to illustrate the subtests are fictitious but they fairly represent those used on the WISC). They are listed from the subtest with the lowest gains over time to the highest. Information has enjoyed a gain of only 2 IQ points while Similarities shows a gain of 24 points.

Information:	On what continent is Argentina?
Arithmetic:	If 4 toys cost 6 dollars, how much do 7 cost?
Vocabulary:	What does "debilitating" mean?
Comprehension:	Why are streets usually numbered in order?
Picture Completion:	Indicate the missing part from an incomplete picture.
Block Design:	Use blocks to replicate a two-color design.
Object Assembly:	Assemble puzzles depicting common objects.
Coding:	Using a key, match symbols with shapes or numbers.
Picture Arrangement:	Reorder a set of scrambled picture cards to tell a story.
Similarities:	In what way are "dogs" and "rabbits" alike?

There is a strong tendency for performance on these ten subtests to be inter-correlated. This means that people who are above average on one of them tend to excel on them all, that is, those who are good at seeing what concepts have in common and good at identifying the missing piece of a pattern tend to be the same people who accumulate large vocabularies, large funds of general information, and arithmetical skills. That is why we speak of a general intelligence factor or g. Naturally, there are other factors: some people are particularly good at the verbal portions of IQ tests, or the quantitative portions, or the items that require spatial visualization. I will largely ignore these subordinate factors because they pose no problem beyond that posed by the g factor.

There is nothing mysterious about the notion of g. In everyday life, all of us talk about general abilities that "lie behind" the fact that someone excels at a wide range of tasks or is superior in a wide range of traits. We talk about good people and mean that there are people who are above average not just in terms of kindness but also in terms of generosity and tolerance, so they have moral g. We have all said of someone that they have athletic ability and meant that they seem to excel at all sports not just at one, so they have athletic g. If someone is good at playing a wide variety of musical instruments, we tend to say that they are "musical," which is to say they have musical g. Similarly, if someone is good at a wide range of cognitively demanding tasks, we say that they have general intelligence or g(IQ).

A mathematical technique called factor analysis measures this tendency of performance on a wide variety of cognitive tasks to be inter-correlated and, technically, g is the quantified result. The g factor explains a surprising amount of individual differences in performance on the WISC subtests, but it is better at predicting performance on some rather than others. This is because good performers consistently open up a larger gap on the average person at some cognitive tasks than others. These tend to be the more cognitively complex tasks, which reinforces the claim of g to be a measure of general intelligence. For example, a high-IQ person excels less on Digit Span forward, which is just remembering numbers in the order in which they were read out, and excels more on Digit Span backward, which is repeating numbers aloud in reverse of the order in which they were read out. The ten WISC subtests can be ranked in terms of their g loadings. That simply means you rank them from the subtest on which high-IQ people beat the average person the most down to the subtest on which they excel the least.

Once again, there is nothing mysterious about various traits or tasks having different g loadings. In the American South of my youth, people who were good tended to be farther above average in terms of kindness than tolerance, which is to say that kindness had a higher g loading than tolerance. Musical people tend to be farther above average on the piano than the drums. A talented cook is likely to exceed me more in making a soufflé than scrambled eggs because the former is more complex than the latter. Therefore, it is a better test of excellence in cooking.

The pervasiveness of the g factor creates certain expectations. If there is such a thing as general intelligence, and if it were to increase over time, we would expect gains on each of the ten WISC subtests to tally with their g loadings. With the exception of Coding, the g loadings are very similar on the various WISC subtests. But when we turn to IQ gains over time, we find something surprising: huge discrepancies between the magnitude of subtest gains and subtest g loadings. For example, Similarities and Information have much the same g loadings, yet the former shows twelve times the gains of the latter. Remember cooking. If cooking skills improved over time, it would be amazing if the g loadings were ignored, for example, if there was a huge gain in scrambling eggs but no gains in making soufflés.

Figure 1 presents a summary of IQ gains in America between 1947 and 2002. The WISC data are most complete for America but I could have chosen another developed nation such as France or Britain. Another test that will be important later is

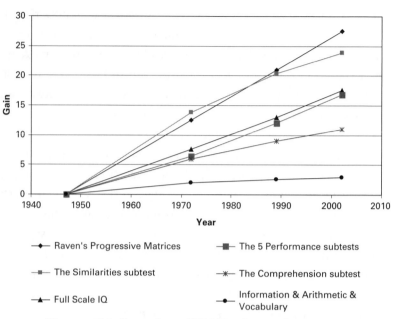

Figure 1 This figure shows WISC IQ gains starting in 1947–1948 and running through 2002. The test was updated three times, which means we get estimates of gains over three periods of 13 to 25 years. All gains are measured in IQ points (with SD set at 15). See Appendix I for Table 1 on which the figure is based. I have also included an "estimate" of American gains on Raven's. There are no reliable US data, but there is a huge literature showing that Raven's gains have proceeded at no less than 0.50 IQ points per year in every developed nation for which we have data. I will list these nations and give the years the data cover:

Belgium: 1958–1967 (Flynn, 1987, Table 2)
Norway: 1954–1980 (Flynn, 1987, Table 4)
The Netherlands: 1952–1982 (Flynn, 1987, Table 1)
Israel: 1971–1984 (Flynn, 1998b, Table 3)
Britain: 1942–1992 (Flynn, 1998a, Figure 3)
Argentina: 1964–1998 (Flynn & Rossi-Casé, under review)

Raven's Progressive Matrices, so I have given a minimal estimate of US gains on Raven's. As the caption to Figure 1 says, there are no good data on Raven's gains in America, so I have used a minimal estimate closely tied to US gains on Similarities. Data from Great

Britain show the two rising in tandem (Flynn, 1998a, Figure 3; Flynn, 2000b, Table 1).

Some trends to note in Figure 1. The various subtests show very different gains: Americans gained 24 points on Similarities between 1947 and 2002 (1.6 SDs), 4 points on Vocabulary, and only 2 points on Arithmetic and Information (for an average of 3 points on these three subtests collectively). The WISC gives not only subtest scores but also a summary judgment on our intelligence called Full Scale IQ. These gains are huge, amounting to about 18 points. The posited gains on Raven's come to fully 27.5 points. How can our recent ancestors have been so unintelligent compared to ourselves? Even worse, we will look at British data that suggest we have to extend these gains all the way back to 1900. So our distant ancestors must have been very stupid indeed. We are now in a position to state three paradoxes and I will throw in a fourth for good measure.

Stating the paradoxes

(1) The factor analysis paradox: how can intelligence be both one and many at the same time or how can IQ gains be so contemptuous of g loadings? How can people get more intelligent and have no larger vocabularies, no larger stores of general information, no greater ability to solve arithmetical problems?

(2) The intelligence paradox: if huge IQ gains are intelligence gains, why are we not stuck by the extraordinary subtlety of our children's conversation? Why do we not have to make allowances for the limitations of our parents? A difference of some 18 points in Full Scale IQ over two generations ought to be highly visible.

(3) The mental retardation (MR) paradox: if we project IQ gains back to 1900, the average IQ scored against current norms was somewhere between 50 and 70. If IQ gains are

in any sense real, we are driven to the absurd conclusion that a majority of our ancestors were mentally retarded. In passing, we are in a transitional period in which the term "mentally retarded" is being replaced by the term "mentally disabled" in the hope of finding words with a less negative connotation. I have retained the old term for clarity and because history has shown that negative connotations are simply passed on from one label to another.

(4) The identical twins paradox: there is no doubt that twins separated at birth, and raised apart, have very similar IQs, presumably because of their identical genes. Indeed a wide range of studies show that genes dominate individual differences in IQ and that environment is feeble. And yet, IQ gains are so great as to signal the existence of environmental factors of enormous potency. How can environment be both so feeble and so potent?

We will address each of these paradoxes in turn but it may help to signal the solutions in shorthand:

(1) The WISC subtests measure a variety of cognitive skills that are functionally independent and responsive to changes in social priorities over time. The inter-correlations that engender g are binding only when comparing individuals within a static social context.

(2) Asking whether IQ gains are intelligence gains is the wrong question because it implies all or nothing cognitive progress. The twentieth century saw some cognitive skills make great gains, while others were in the doldrums. To assess cognitive trends, we must dissect "intelligence" into solving mathematical problems, interpreting the great works of literature, finding on-the-spot solutions, assimilating the scientific worldview, critical acumen, and wisdom.

(3) Our ancestors in 1900 were not mentally retarded. Their intelligence was anchored in everyday reality. We differ

from them in that we can use abstractions and logic and the hypothetical to attack the formal problems that arise when science liberates thought from concrete situations. Since 1950, we have become more ingenious in going beyond previously learned rules to solve problems on the spot.

(4) At a given time, genetic differences between individuals (within an age cohort) are dominant but only because they have hitched powerful environmental factors to their star. Trends over time (between cohorts) liberate environmental factors from the sway of genes and, once unleashed, they can have a powerful cumulative effect.

Swimming freely of g

I fear that I have a taste for sports analogies. If we factor analyzed performances on the ten events of the decathlon, a general factor or g would emerge and, no doubt, subordinate factors representing speed (the sprints), spring (jumping events), and strength (throwing events). We would get a g(D) because, at a given time and place, performance on the ten events would be inter-correlated, that is, someone who tended to be superior on any one would tend to be above average on all. We would also get various g loadings for the ten events, that is, superior performers would tend to rise farther above average on some of them than on the others. The 100 meters would have a much higher g loading than the 1,500 meters, which involves an endurance factor not very necessary in the other events.

Decathlon g might well have much utility in predicting performance differences between athletes of the same age cohort. However, if we used it to predict progress over time and forecast that trends on the ten events would move in tandem, we would go astray. That is because g(D) cannot discriminate between pairs of events in terms of the extent to which they are functionally related.

Let us assume that the 100 meters, the hurdles, and the high jump all had large and similar g loadings as they almost certainly would. A sprinter needs upper-body strength as well as speed, a hurdler needs speed and spring, a high jumper needs spring and timing. I have no doubt that a good athlete would best the average athlete handily on all three at a given place and time. However, over time, social priorities change. People become obsessed with the 100 meters as the most spectacular spectator event (the world's fastest human). Young people find success in this event a secondary sexual characteristic of great allure. Over thirty years, performance escalates by a full SD in the 100 meters, by half an SD in the hurdles, and not at all in the high jump.

In sum, the trends do not mimic the relative g loadings of the "subtests." One pair of events highly correlated (sprint and hurdles) shows a modest trend for both to move in the same direction and another pair equally highly correlated (sprint and high jump) shows trends greatly at variance. At the end of the thirty years, we do another factor analysis of performance on the ten events of the decathlon and, lo and behold, g(D) is still there. Although average performance has risen "eccentrically" on various events, the following is still true: superior performers still do better than average on all ten events and are about the same degree above average on various events as they were thirty years before.

Factor loadings have proved deceptive about whether various athletic skills are functionally independent. We can react to this in two ways: either confront the surprising autonomy of various skills and seek a solution by depth analysis of how they function in the real world; or deny that anything real has happened and classify the trends over time as artifacts. The second option is respectable if you can actually present evidence. Perhaps the sprinters of thirty years ago lacked "event sophistication": they may have been so tense at the starting line that they all got slow starts when the gun went off. Perhaps the content of the event used to disadvantage sprinters by way of "cultural bias": the starters may have been Etonians (my word processor wants me to say Estonians) who insisted on issuing their commands in Greek. Such things would mean that better 100 meters times do not signal any real increase in speed. Therefore, the problems of why there has been only a moderate carry over to the hurdles and why there has been no carry over to the high jump are pseudo-problems.

But if there is no such evidence, the second option is sterile. It becomes a matter of saying that since the trends are not factor invariant, they must be artifacts. This assumes that the hypotheses about functional skills in the real world that factor analysis poses need not be tested against evidence. Or that evidence cannot be real evidence if it is falsifying. I assume that this is an option no one will choose.

It is better to talk to some athletics coaches. They tell us that over the years, everyone has become focused on the 100 meters and it is hard to get people to take other events seriously. They point out that sprint speed may be highly correlated with high jump performance but, past a certain point, it is actually counterproductive. If you hurl yourself at the bar at maximum speed, your forward momentum cannot be converted into upward lift and you are likely to time your jump badly. They are not surprised that increased sprint speed has made some contribution to the hurdles because speed between the hurdles is important. But it is only half the story: you have to control your speed so that you take the same number of steps between hurdles and always jump off the same foot. If you told these coaches that you found it surprising that real-world shifts in priorities, and the real-world functional relationships between events, ignored the factor loadings of the events, I think they would find your mindset surprising.

Back to the WISC subtests. Arithmetic, Information, Vocabulary, and Similarities all load heavily on g(IQ) and on a shared verbal factor. Despite this, as we saw in Figure 1, Americans gained 24 points on Similarities between 1947 and 2002, 4 points on

Vocabulary, and only 2 points on Arithmetic and Information. Which is to say that the pattern of gains bears little relation to factor loadings and cannot qualify as factor invariant. However, as usual, factor analysis was done in a static setting where individuals were compared and social change was absent. It has no necessary applicability to the dynamic scenario of social priorities altering over time. Therefore, the factor loadings adduced can at best pose hypotheses to be tested against the evidence of actual score trends over time. And g(IQ) turns out to be a bad guide as to which real-world cognitive skills are merely correlated and which are functionally related.

The artifact option cannot be supported by evidence. Test sophistication has to do with feeling comfortable with the format of IQ tests, or whoever administers them, or using your time better, or trying harder in the test room. The twentieth century saw us go from subjects who had never taken a standardized test to people bombarded by them, and, undoubtedly, a small portion of gains in the first half of the century was due to growing test sophistication. Since 1947, its role has been relatively modest. US gains have been steady at least since 1932 (Flynn, 1984b). Which is to say that they antedate the period when testing was common, were robust while testing was at its maximum, and have persisted into an era when IQ testing waned, due to its growing unpopularity.

If gains are due to test sophistication, they should show a certain pattern. When naive subjects are first exposed to IQ tests, they gain a few points but, after that, repeated exposures show sharply diminished returns. America has been waiting for at least seventy years for its rate of gain to diminish. Other nations show accelerating gains over an extended period. For example, in the Netherlands, a huge rate of gain escalated decade after decade from 1952 to 1982 (Flynn, 1987).

Are IQ gains due to "cultural bias"? We must distinguish between cultural trends that render neutral content more familiar and cultural trends that really raise the level of cognitive skills. If the spread of the scientific ethos has made people capable of using logic to attack a wider range of problems, that is a real gain in cognitive skills. If no one has taken the trouble to update the words on a vocabulary test to eliminate those that have gone out of everyday usage, then an apparent score loss is ersatz. I can discern no cultural bias that favors the present generation. Note that obsolete items would actually lead to an underestimate of IQ gains. We measure IQ gains in terms of the extent to which people do better on a old test unchanged from twenty-five years before their time (say the WISC) than they do on a more current test whose content has been updated (say the WISC-R).

Let us supply a tentative functional analysis of various cognitive skill trends over time that explains their pattern without downgrading their reality. Assume for the moment (evidence below) that science has engendered a sea change. We no longer use our minds to solve problems on a concrete level only; rather we also use them to solve problems on a formal level. Once we used logic primarily with concrete referents: all toadstools are poisonous; that is a toadstool; therefore, it is poisonous. Now we have become accustomed to using logic with the general categories provided by science: only mammals bear their young alive; rabbits and dogs both bear their young alive; therefore, they are both mammals.

I will show that this would bring huge gains over time on a subtest like Similarities. But so long as other subtests sampled the core vocabulary and information needed in everyday life, this causal factor would not trigger large gains on those subtests. Indeed, changing social priorities might include both emphasis on a more scientific outlook and less time for reading, in which case huge Similarities gains could be accompanied by Vocabulary and Information losses. All of these real-world functional skills would assert their autonomy from one another and from the straitjacket of factor loadings.

Arithmetic deserves special mention because some have confused mathematical thinking with the cognitive problems posed by Raven's Progressive Matrices. This is a test that offers a

Box 2

Here is an item very like those found on the Raven's Progressive Matrices test.

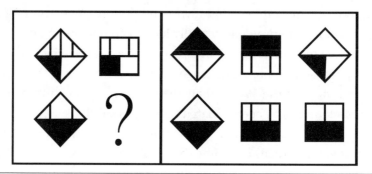

design with a piece missing and six to eight "pictures," one of which is the missing piece. You have to select the piece that fits, and this involves noting similarities and differences across the rows and down the columns of the design. Look at the item in Box 2. You can immediately see that the missing piece must be square. Then you note that the bottom half of the square will have to be solid black; and that the top half should be divided into only two parts. So the missing piece and right answer must be the square on the lower right.

Raven's demands that you think out problems on the spot without a previously learned method for doing so, and mathematics requires mastering new proofs dealing with non-verbal material. Therefore, the fact that they are highly correlated in terms of factor loadings seems to signal that they require similar cognitive skills. Therefore, it seems sensible to teach young children Raven's-type problems in the hope that they will become better mathematics problem solvers. Indeed, US schools have been doing that since 1991 (Blair, Gamson, Thorne, & Baker, 2005, pp. 100–101).

Here IQ gains over time not only trump factor analysis but also validate their credentials as a diagnostician of functional relationships between cognitive skills. The large gains on Raven's and virtually nil gains on Arithmetic show that the relationship between the two is no more functional than the relationship between sprinting and the high jump. Sadly, our understanding of the functional process for learning arithmetic is far behind our understanding of the high jump. Some speculation: except for mathematicians who link the formulae with proofs, mathematics is less a logical enterprise than a separate reality with its own laws that are at variance with those of the natural world. Therefore, just as infants explore the natural world, children must explore the world of mathematics themselves and become familiar with its "objects" by self-discovery.

Michael Shayer is breaking new ground using teaching techniques based on self-discovery within small groups. In addition, he may have found cognitive skills that have genuine functional links to arithmetical reasoning. In Britain from 1975 to 2003, performance among schoolchildren on the Piagetian tasks of conceptualizing volume and heaviness declined by 0.8 SDs. Flynn (under review) has analyzed British WISC data covering the latter half of that period. From 1990 to 2003, British children lost 0.4 SDs on the WISC Arithmetic subtest. The rates of loss are of course identical (Shayer & Adhami, 2003; Shayer & Adhami, in press; Shayer, Ginsberg, & Coe, in press).

To sum up, factor analysis and g(IQ) describe a static situation where individual differences are compared and social change is frozen. The degree to which superior people are above average on the various subtests sets their respective g loadings. IQ gains over time describe a dynamic situation in which social priorities shift in a multitude of ways: no better math teachers, more leisure but with the extra leisure devoted to visual rather then verbal pursuits, the spread of the scientific ethos, and a host of other things all occurring together. The average on Similarities rises but the average on Arithmetic and Vocabulary does not. How odd it would be if social trends mimicked factor loadings in

17

determining what real-world cognitive skills progress and which mark time! If they did so, IQ gains would appear factor invariant, but that would be purely accidental (Wicherts *et al.*, 2004). Although radically different trends alter average performances on various WISC subtests between Time 1 and Time 2, note that this leaves a certain stability untouched. Superior performers are much the same degree above average on each and every subtest at both Time 2 and Time 1. Therefore, much the same g will emerge.

A final attempt to shake those resistant to this analysis. Imagine we had a test of occupational performance where everyone took three subtests: they all spent six months as a tutor, six months filing documents, and six months as a messenger. Some people tend to do better at all three so a g emerges. Those who do better exceed the average most at tutoring, next at filing, and least at delivering messages, so the g loadings run from highest to lowest in that order. Over time, thanks to visual culture, there is no gain in verbal fluency but map-reading skills improve. Therefore, when the test is administered thirty years later, there are messenger gains but no tutoring gains, in defiance of the g loadings. Is there anything really surprising about that?

Our first paradox is resolved. At any particular time, factor analysis will extract g(IQ) – and intelligence appears unitary. Over time, real-world cognitive skills assert their functional autonomy and swim freely of g – and intelligence appears multiple. If you want to see g, stop the film and extract a snapshot; you will not see it while the film is running. Society does not do factor analysis. It is a juggernaut that flattens factor loadings and imposes its own priorities.

Where has all of the intelligence gone?

As Figure 1 showed, Full Scale IQ gains in America are impressive. I am a grandparent and a member of the WISC generation who were aged 5 to 15 when they were tested in 1947–1948.

Let us put our IQ at 100. Our children are essentially the WISC-R generation who were 6 to 16 when tested in 1972 and, against the WISC norms, their mean IQ was almost 108. Our grandchildren are the WISC-IV generation who were 6 to 16 in 2002 and, against the WISC norms, their IQ was almost 118. We can of course work backward rather then forward. If the present generation is put at 100, their grandparents had a mean IQ of 82. Either today's children are so bright that they should run circles around us, or their grandparents were so dull that it is surprising that they could keep a modern society ticking over.

In either event, the cognitive gulf between the generations should be huge. Taking the second scenario, almost 20 percent of my generation would have had an IQ of 70 or below and be eligible to be classed as mentally retarded. Over 60 percent of American blacks would have been MR. Anyone born before 1940 knows that all of this is absurd.

The solution to the paradox is to be found not by focusing on Full Scale IQ trends, but by focusing on the WISC subtest trends plus Raven's trends. As we saw in Figure 1, between 1947 (WISC) and 2002 (WISC-IV), Similarities and Raven's show huge gains of 24 to 27 points (SD = 15), the five Performance subtests show gains averaging 17 points, Comprehension shows 11 points, and the remaining Verbal subtests (Information, Arithmetic, and Vocabulary) show very limited gains averaging 3 points. Let us continue our analysis of the cognitive skills needed to do well on the various IQ subtests and compare their trends with trends on tests of educational achievement.

The huge Raven's gains show that today's children are far better at solving problems on the spot without a previously learned method for doing so. The WISC Performance subtests all measure this to some degree. They require arranging blocks so that the view from above duplicates a presented pattern, building an object out of its disassembled parts, arranging pictures to tell a story. On the other hand, most children have some prior experience at jigsaw puzzles or reading books in which pictures are the main vehicle of the story. I suspect that the fact that the on-the-spot element is diluted in the Performance subtests explains why their gains, although substantial, lag behind Raven's gains.

We turn to the subtests that show minimal gains. Having an adequate fund of general information, having a decent vocabulary, and being able to do arithmetic are very close to school-taught skills. As far as Information and Vocabulary are concerned, it is less a matter of solving problems on the spot than exhibiting what you know: you either know that Rome is the capital of Italy or you know only of Rome, Georgia; you know what "delectable" means or you do not.

It is illuminating to use their trends to analyze trends on the National Association of Educational Progress (NAEP) tests, often called the Nation's Report Card. The NAEP tests are administered to large representative samples of fourth, eighth, and twelfth graders. From 1971 to 2002, fourth and eighth graders (average age 11 years old) made a reading gain equivalent to almost 4 IQ points. However, by the twelfth grade, the reading gain drops off to almost nothing (US Department of Education, 2000, pp. 104 and 110; 2003, p. 21).

The IQ data suggest an interesting possibility. For the sake of comparability, we will focus on WISC trends from 1972 to 2002, rather than on the full period beginning in 1947. Between 1972 and 2002, US schoolchildren made no gain in their store of general information and only minimal vocabulary gains. Therefore, while today's children may learn to master pre-adult literature at a younger age, they are no better prepared for reading more demanding adult literature. You cannot enjoy *War and Peace* if you have to run to the dictionary or encyclopedia every other paragraph. Take Kipling's poem:

> Over the Kremlin's serpentine pavement white
> Strode five generals

Each simultaneously taking snuff
Which softness itself was yet the stuff
To leave the grand white neck no gash
Where a chain might snap

If you do not know what the Kremlin is, or what "serpentine" means, or that taking snuff involves using a snuff rag, you will hardly realize that these generals caught the Czar unaware and strangled him.

In other words, today's schoolchildren opened up an early lead on their grandparents by learning the mechanics of reading at an earlier age. But by age 17, their grandparents had caught up. And since current students are no better than their grandparents in terms of vocabulary and general information, the two generations at 17 are dead equal in their ability to read the adult literature expected of a senior in high school.

From 1973 to 2000, the Nation's Report Card shows fourth and eighth graders making mathematics gains equivalent to almost 7 IQ points. These put the young children of today at the 68th percentile of their parents' generation. But once again, the gain falls off at the twelfth grade, this time to literally nothing (US Department of Education, 2000, pp. 54 and 60–61; 2001, p. 24). And once again, a WISC subtest suggests why.

The Arithmetic subtest and the NAEP mathematics tests present a composite picture. An increasing percentage of young children have been mastering the computational skills the Nation's Report Card emphasizes at those ages. However, the WISC Arithmetic subtest measures both computational skills and something extra. The questions are put verbally and often in a context that requires more than a times-table-type answer. For example, take an item like: "if 4 toys cost 6 dollars, how much do 7 cost?" Many subjects who can do straight paper calculations cannot diagnose the two operations required: that you must first divide and then multiply. Others cannot do mental arithmetic involving fractions. In other words, WISC Arithmetic also tests for the kind of mind that is likely to be able to reason mathematically.

My hypothesis is that during the period in which children mastered calculating skills at an earlier age, they made no progress in acquiring mathematical reasoning skills. Note the minimal gains registered on WISC Arithmetic (see Appendix I, Table 1: 1972 to 2002). Reasoning skills are essential for higher mathematics. Therefore, by the twelfth grade, the failure to develop enhanced mathematical problem-solving strategies begins to bite. American schoolchildren cannot do algebra and geometry any better than the previous generation. Once again, although the previous generation were slower to master computational skills, they were no worse off at graduation.

Recall that the failure of secondary students to better their parents is qualified by one important exception. Today's youth are much better at on-the-spot problem solving without a previously learned method. It is likely that this advantage is sustained and perhaps enhanced by university study. There are a number of likely dividends. Every year America has an increased number of managerial, professional, and technical jobs to fill – jobs that often require decisions without the guidance of set rules.

Although we have focused on post-1972 subtest trends, these are virtually identical with post-1947 trends. And we now know why recent IQ gains do not imply that today's young people would put their grandparents to shame. Assume we hear a recent high-school graduate chatting with his grandfather (who also finished high school) about a novel they both read the week before. There is no reason to believe either would have to make any allowance for the obtuseness of the other. Assume we discover essays on current affairs they both wrote shortly after graduation. There is no reason to believe that either would strike us as inferior to the other in terms of vocabulary or fund of general information.

We would be likely to notice some differences. The grandson would be much better in terms of on-the-spot problem solving in certain contexts. He would be no more innovative in solving mechanical problems such as fixing a car or repairing things around the house. But he would be more adept at dealing with novel problems posed verbally or visually or abstractly. Sometimes, the grandfather's "handicap" would affect social conversation, particularly because he would not think that such problems were very important. The grandfather might be more rule-governed and would probably count that as a virtue.

Distant ancestors: Similarities

The grandparents of today's children were assigned a median birth date of 1937 to get them in school in time for the WISC. But what of their parents and grandparents, what of the cohort that was born in 1907 and the even more distant cohort born in 1877? British Raven's data show massive gains beginning with those born in 1877 – they were actually tested at maturity of course. World War I military data show that US gains were under way as far back as we can measure (Raven, Raven, & Court, 1993, Graph G2; Tuddenham, 1948).

The Wechsler–Binet rate of gain (0.30 points per year) entails that the schoolchildren of 1900 would have had a mean IQ just under 70. The Raven–Similarities rate (0.50 points per year) yields a mean IQ of 50 (against current norms). The latter is particularly disturbing. It will hardly do to simply say that our ancestors were bad at on-the-spot problem solving. After all, innovative thinking is an important real-world skill. Only the worst of the 2,200 schoolchildren used to norm the WISC-IV would have performed as low as the average child of 1900.

To make our ancestors that lacking in problem-solving initiative is to turn them into virtual automatons. Moreover, there is some connection between mental acuity and the ability to learn. Jensen (1981, p. 65) relates an interview with a young man with a Wechsler IQ of 75. Despite the fact that he attended baseball games frequently, he was vague about the rules, did not know how many players were on a team, could not name the teams his home team played, and could not name any of the most famous players.

When Americans attended baseball games a century ago, were almost half of them too dull to follow the game or use a scorecard? My father who was born in 1885 taught me to keep score and spoke as if this was something virtually everyone did when he was a boy. How did Englishmen play cricket in 1900? Taking their mean IQ at face value, most of them would need a minder to position them in the field, tell them when to bat, and tell them when the innings was over.

The solution to this paradox rests on two distinctions that explain in turn the huge and therefore embarrassing gains made on the Similarities subtest and Raven's. The first distinction is that between pre-scientific and post-scientific operational thinking. A person who views the world through pre-scientific spectacles thinks in terms of the categories that order perceived objects and functional relationships. When presented with a Similarities-type item such as "what do dogs and rabbits have in common," Americans in 1900 would be likely to say, "You use dogs to hunt rabbits." The correct answer, that they are both mammals, assumes that the important thing about the world is to classify it in terms of the categories of science. Even if the subject were aware of those categories, the correct answer would seem absurdly trivial. Who cares that they are both mammals? That is the least important thing about them from his point of view. What is important is orientation in space and time, what things are useful, and what things are under one's control, that is, what does one possess.

The hypothesis is that our ancestors found pre-scientific spectacles more comfortable than post-scientific spectacles, that is, pre-scientific spectacles showed them what they considered to be most important about the world. If the everyday world is your cognitive home, it is not natural to detach abstractions and logic and the hypothetical from their concrete referents. It is not that pre-scientific people did not use abstractions: the concept of hunting as distinct from fishing is an abstraction. They would use syllogistic logic all of the time: Basset hounds are good for hunting; that is a Basset hound; that dog would be good at hunting. They would of course use the hypothetical: if I had two dogs rather than only one, I could catch more rabbits. But the reference is always to the concrete relationships that dominate the everyday world.

Today we have no difficulty freeing logic from concrete referents and reasoning about purely hypothetical situations. People were not always thus. Christopher Hallpike (1979) and Nick Mackintosh (2006) have drawn my attention to the seminal book on the social foundations of cognitive development by Luria (1976). His interviews with peasants in remote areas of the Soviet Union offer some wonderful examples. The dialogues paraphrased run as follows:

White bears and Novaya Zemlya (pp. 108–109)

Q: All bears are white where there is always snow; in Novaya Zemlya there is always snow; what color are the bears there?

A: I have seen only black bears and I do not talk of what I have not seen.

Q: But what do my words imply?

A: If a person has not been there he can not say anything on the basis of words. If a man was 60 or 80 and had seen a white bear there and told me about it, he could be believed.

Camels and Germany (p. 112)

Q: There are no camels in Germany; the city of B is in Germany; are there camels there or not?

A: I don't know, I have never seen German villages. If B is a large city, there should be camels there.

Q: But what if there aren't any in all of Germany?

A: If B is a village, there is probably no room for camels.

The peasants are entirely correct. They understand the difference between analytic and synthetic propositions: pure logic cannot tell us anything about facts; only experience can. But this will do them no good on current IQ tests. As for the effect of attachment to the concrete on classification, the kind of thing required in the Similarities subtest, Luria (1976) serves to drive the point home.

Dogs and chickens (pp. 81–82)
Q: What do a chicken and a dog have in common?
A: They are not alike. A chicken has two legs, a dog has four. A chicken has wings but a dog doesn't. A dog has big ears and a chicken's are small.
Q: Is there one word you could use for them both?
A: No, of course not.
Q: Would the word "animal" fit?
A: Yes.

Fish and crows (p. 82)
Q: What do a fish and a crow have in common?
A: A fish – it lives in water. A crow flies. If the fish just lies on top of the water, the crow could peck at it. A crow can eat a fish but a fish can't eat a crow.
Q: Could you use one word for them both?
A: If you call them "animals," that wouldn't be right. A fish isn't an animal and a crow isn't either. A crow can eat a fish but a fish can't eat a bird. A person can eat a fish but not a crow.

Note that even after an abstract term is suggested, that kind of answer is still alien. Today we are so familiar with the categories of science that it seems obvious that the most important attribute things have in common is that they are both animate, or mammals, or chemical compounds. However, people attached to the concrete will not find those categories natural at all. First, they will be far more reluctant to classify. Second, when they do classify, they will have a strong preference for concrete similarities (two things look alike, two animals are functionally related, for example, one eats the other) over a similarity in terms of abstract categories. The Similarities subtest assumes exactly the opposite, that is, it damns the concrete in favor of the abstract. The WISC scoring directions assume this principle and the WISC-R makes it explicit (Wechsler, 1974, p. 155). References to items still in use have been deleted and italics are mine:

> *Pertinent* general categorizations are given 2 points, while the naming of one or more common properties or functions of a member of a pair (a more *concrete* problem-solving approach) merits only 1 point. Thus, stating that a pound and a yard are "Both measures" (their general category) earns a higher score than saying "You can measure things with them" (a main function of each). Similarly calling something a "feeling" is *less concrete* (and worth a higher score) than "the way you feel." Of course, even a relatively *concrete* approach, to solving the items ... requires the child to abstract something similar about the members of the pair. Some children are unable to do this, and may respond to each member separately rather than to the pair as a whole ... Although such a response is a true statement, it is scored 0 because it does not give a similarity.

The preference for answers that classify the world (and extra credit for the vocabulary of science) is extraordinary and reaches an even higher level in the WISC-IV, where the "1 point" for concrete answers is reduced to "merits no or only a partial credit" (Psychological Corporation, 2003, p. 71). This preference dominates the specific scoring directions given item by item. I have used a fictitious item (dogs and rabbits) to illustrate the point, but an item abandoned after the WISC-R will show that I am not exaggerating. "What do liberty and justice have in common?": 2 points for the answer that both are ideals or that both are moral rights, 1 point for both are freedoms, 0 for both are what we have in America. The examiner is told that "freedoms" gets 1 point while "free things" gets 0 because the latter is a more concrete response (Wechsler, 1974, p. 159). You are just not supposed to be preoccupied with how we use something or how much good it does you to possess it.

Even in 1900, American children were not immersed in the everyday world to the same extent as Soviet peasants. However, it is likely they still used pre-scientific spectacles more often than post-scientific ones and if so, it is hard to see how they could get more than half credit on the typical Similarities item. If the children of 1900 were given a prehistoric version of the WISC-IV, they would have a raw score ceiling of 22. This is at the 25th percentile of contemporary children aged 14. The average child of 1900 would have a raw score of about 11 and be two SDs below the current mean, which translates into an IQ score of 70 against today's norms (Psychological Corporation, 2003, p. 229). This was the "target" score that Full Scale IQ gains implied when projected back to 1900. But recall that Similarities sets the more demanding target of a mean IQ of 50. It looks as if the permeation of our minds by scientific categories has been supplemented by additional factors as yet unknown. It cannot be the influence of a more visual culture because Similarities items are posed verbally. Or perhaps the projection of Similarities gains at the post-1947 rate back to the turn of the century is unwarranted.

Note how the WISC manuals use the word "pertinent" to justify rewarding "general categories." This is just a synonym for claiming that classification is what is important about a pair of things. Imagine a rural child in 1900 being told that the most important thing about dogs and rabbits is a name that applies to both, rather than what you use them for. These comments are not a criticism of the architects of the WISC-IV. Today, when all children are being schooled in a scientific era, the brighter child probably will be the one who uses the categories and vocabulary

Box 3

If people have adopted the language of science and use logic and the hypothetical freely, why do so many of them believe nonsense about the Loch Ness monster, flying saucers, astrology, and so forth? The answer is that scientific language and abstract argument can be used just as easily to defend nonsense as sense, witness "creation science." The vocabulary and habits of mind fostered by science do not automatically engender critical acumen or wisdom. They provide a foundation but much has to be done to build a temple of reason on that foundation. Chapter 7 will discuss all of this in detail.

of science. But what we need not infer is this: that the huge gains on Similarities from one generation to another signal a general lack of intelligence on the part of our ancestors. Their minds were simply not permeated by scientific language and they were not in the habit of reasoning beyond the concrete.

This solution to our paradox does not imply that massive IQ gains over time are trivial. They represent nothing less than a liberation of the human mind. The scientific ethos, with its vocabulary, taxonomies, and detachment of logic and the hypothetical from concrete referents, has begun to permeate the minds of post-industrial people. This has paved the way for mass education on the university level and the emergence of an intellectual cadre without whom our present civilization would be inconceivable (but do not expect too much – see Box 3).

The fact that we now use our intelligence in a new way does not mean, of course, that we use it any less in dealing with the concrete problems we encounter in everyday life. It is just that more formal schooling and the nature of our leisure activities have altered the balance between the abstract and concrete. The life experiences that surround us pose problems largely absent in our ancestors' day.

Distant ancestors: Raven's

The above distinction is relevant to Raven's Progressive Matrices in that the entire test demands detaching logic from a concrete referent. However, when challenged by examination conditions, even subjects unused to this can adapt to varying degrees. I believe we can get more precision about the extent to which our distant ancestors were handicapped by calling upon Piaget, that is, his distinction between concrete and formal thinking.

First, I will try to show that being on the concrete level handicaps one for performing the sort of tasks posed by IQ tests and yet carries no implication of mental retardation. Second, I will argue for a connection between viewing the world through pre-scientific spectacles and the concrete level with the implication that most people were on the concrete level in 1900. Third, I will show how that hypothesis could account for the performance gap on Raven's that separates us from our distant ancestors.

Trevor Bond has developed Bond's Logical Operations Test (the BLOT) to distinguish whether someone uses logic on a concrete or formal level (Endler & Bond, 2006). Two items illustrate the threshold between the two:

> (I) A boy has a constant weight for six months. He decided to swim 4 miles a day (on top of his normal activities) to train for the state swimming titles. If he wants to keep his weight the same he will have to: (a) keep his food level the same; (b) eat more food; (c) eat less food; (d) exercise more.

The correct answer, of course, is "eat more food." It seems obvious to us (I suspect all of my readers are on the formal level) but many adolescents cannot get it. It involves abstracting from the concrete situation a series of "equations" about weight: constant weight = consistent input of food + exercise; more exercise = weight loss; therefore, more food is needed because that = weight gain (operation of identity).

(II) A young woman has kept her weight at a constant level over the past six months. Which of the following would cause her weight to change a lot? (a) eating less food and doing less exercise; (b) increasing food eaten and increasing exercise taken; (c) eating and exercising at the same level as always; (d) eating at the same level and exercising more.

The correct answer is "eating at the same level and exercising more." It will seem surprising that some people can do (I) correctly but not (II). But in (II), you have a more cognitively complex task: you have to discern what combination of food and exercise will cause weight to either rise or fall (operation of reciprocity).

Are people who cannot operate on the formal level mentally retarded? That can hardly be so because a sizable percentage of today's teenagers have not attained that level. This will come as a surprise to those who have read Piaget; but today, there is general agreement that Piaget worked with an elite sample of children, put the ages at which children attain the formal mode far too low, and did not allow for the historical context as a determinant of whether children would reach the formal level at all. Flieller (1999) presents trends for French 14-year-olds on a test that measures a broad range of Piagetian tasks. He puts 35 percent of them at the formal level in 1967 and 55 percent in 1996. Shayer, Küchemann, and Wylam (1976) tested only for those Piagetian tasks having to do with assessing heaviness and volume. They found that in the mid 1970s, 20 percent of British children aged 14 had attained the formal level. Shayer and Adhami (2003) argue that British children have lost ground since then. Clearly, national honor is at stake (see Box 4).

If we put the percentage of American teenagers who cannot do Bond's items (I) and (II) as the bottom 50 percent, it is clear that most of them are not incapable of dealing with everyday life. They would know enough to diet to lower their weight. They could train sensibly for the state swimming championships. People

Box 4

As we have seen, the British losses in assessing heaviness and volume were accompanied by losses on the WISC Arithmetic subtest and I have hypothesized a functional link between the two. But what we really need to do is amass the evidence that would allow us to link all of the various Piagetian tasks to various WISC subtests, preferably by finding a consistent international pattern of corresponding losses and gains. At present, the necessary Piagetian data simply do not exist.

below the formal level in 1900 would have been even more competent. Formal schooling is highly correlated with Piagetian progress. Today's 14-year-olds live at a time in which they have had nine years of formal schooling with more to come. In the America of 1900, adults had an average of about seven years of schooling, a median of six and a half years, and 25 percent had completed four years or less (Folger & Nam, 1967). And it was schooling of much inferior quality.

Equally important, the bottom half of today's teenagers cannot extract Bond's general rules from concrete reality, despite living in a scientific age. Virtually all people in 1900 lived in a pre-scientific age. This is not to say that the distinction between concrete vs. formal is identical to the distinction between pre-scientific vs. post-scientific. It is quite possible to extract and manipulate proper equations about what will increase your weight and still tend to use pre-scientific rather than post-scientific categories to classify the world around you. However, the two are undoubtedly causally linked in terms of historical context. People lacking a scientific perspective are much more likely to have their intelligence grounded on the concrete level.

No one can go back to 1900 and give Piagetian tests. I merely assert the following as a plausible hypothesis: most people were on the concrete level in 1900; a majority of people today move to the formal level in their early teens and, by adulthood, they are over-whelmingly on the formal level.

How much relevance does the concrete/formal distinction have to performance on Raven's? Andrich and Styles (1994) did a five-year study of the intellectual development of children initially 10, 12, and 14 years of age. From the parent sample of 201 children, Styles (in press) selected sixty children who were representative of the larger group on the basis of age and initial testing. They took both a Piagetian test and items from Raven's ranked in order of difficulty. Over a period of four years, they were tested yearly on the former and twice yearly on the latter.

Recall what Raven's Progressive Matrices is like (look back to Box 2). It presents the subject with patterns each of which has a piece missing. Six (or eight) alternatives picture a candidate for the missing piece and the subject must select the one that fits the logic of the matrix design. There are sixty items on Raven's. Five Raven's items were used to illustrate the sections of the test and, therefore, were automatic correct answers. Two items were so easy for this group of children that everyone got them correct. The remaining fifty-three items mapped on to ascending Piagetian competence in ascending order of difficulty. Of these, twenty required the subject to be either on the threshold of the formal level or operating on that level. As Styles says, these items require using either a number of rules or a very complex rule to interpret the matrix pattern; and the subject needs to consider the logical relations between rela-tions, rather than the stand-alone relationship between a proposi-tion and concrete reality.

In other words, if people in 1900 were primarily on the concrete level, we would expect their raw scores to have a ceiling of about 40. John Raven (2000, p. RS3 18) established norms for the US circa 1982 and these show a raw score of 40 at the 38th percentile of 14-year-olds. The age curve corresponding to a ceiling of 40 is that of 7.5-year-olds. Their median is a score of 20, which is off the bot-tom of the curve for 14-year-olds. So Raven's gains between 1900 and

2000 can be as large as you wish without any presumption that most of our ancestors suffered from MR. They were quite capable of on-the-spot problem solving in the concrete situations that dominated their lives. The ingenuity of soldiers trying to stay alive in the trenches of World War I and the improvisations of mechanics trying to keep the first motorcars running are part of the historical record.

In stating my solution to the third paradox, I have spoken with the assurance of someone on fire with new ideas. Others may well come forward with alternatives. I urge only that they keep the parameters of the paradox in mind – our ancestors were not mentally retarded; yet they could not cope with a huge number of Raven's items; nor could they, as recently as those born in the 1930s, cope with a large number of Similarities items – and that we must seek an explanation in new habits of mind, rather than talk about test sophistication.

Similarities and Raven's

Until recently, I was deceived about the cognitive tasks set by Similarities. There are a few items that require you to solve problems on the spot without a previously learned method. When asked: "How are dawn and dusk alike?", children have to imagine alternatives and select the one that best catches an intrinsic similarity. Something like: "You get up in the morning and go to bed at night but that makes no sense because I often sleep past dawn and go to bed after dark. They are alike in that the sky is half-lit and often very pretty but of course that is not always true. What they really have in common is that they are the beginning and end of both the day and the night. The right answer must be that they separate day and night."

But almost all of the items on Similarities do not really require this kind of thinking. Some merely require habitual use of the vocabulary of science. When asked why dogs and rabbits are alike, a modern child does not need to reflect very much to answer that they are both mammals. Others merely require a mind focused on classifying the world in terms of abstract categories.

I can now understand something about these two tests that always puzzled me and led me into error (Flynn, 2006a). Why does performance on Similarities correlate so well with performance on Raven's? Case, Demetriou, Platsidou, and Katz (2001) analyzed twenty-three tests including both traditional psychometric items (Matrices, seven WISC subtests, and so forth) and Piagetian tasks (tilted boxes task, weights task, class inclusion, etc.). They found that Matrices and Similarities were similar in the sense that they had virtually identical loadings as measures of fluid intelligence.

Yet, as we have seen, Raven's measures on-the-spot problem solving in the sense of diagnosing the logic of matrices patterns, while Similarities measures primarily competence in classifying. The solution to the puzzle is one that is by now familiar. The same sort of person will do well on both tests, namely, someone whose mind has been liberated from the concrete. That is enough to establish a correlation. There is no need for a significant functional connection between what a person does on the two tests. The cognitive tasks set by one need not be similar to the cognitive tasks set by the other.

Note how little information is conveyed by the fact that they both load highly on fluid g. That is true and it does convey that the performance of a person on one will be a good predictor of performance on the other. But it tells us nothing about a deeper truth. The reason score gains over time occur on both is due to a common causal factor: minds influenced by the scientific ethos find both tests congenial.

The heritability of basketball

There have been many TV documentaries about identical twins who despite being separated at birth, have had amazingly similar life experiences and grow up to have similar IQs. These studies are interpreted as showing that genetic influences on IQ are potent and environmental influences feeble. Studies of identical twins raised apart are only one component of a wide variety of kinship studies. There have been comparisons of identical and fraternal twins each brought up by their own parents, comparisons of adopted children with natural children, and so forth. Most psychologists agree in the interpretation of these studies. For example, Jensen (1998) concludes that while environment may have some potency at earlier ages, IQ differences between adults are overwhelmingly determined by genetic differences.

And yet, how is this possible? As we have seen, there are massive IQ differences between one generation and another. No one has been selectively breeding human beings for high IQ, so it looks as if genetic differences between the generations would be trivial (we will evidence that assumption in Chapter 5). If that is so, environmental factors must cause IQ gains over time and, given the size of those gains, those environmental factors must have enormous potency. How can solid evidence show that environment is both feeble (kinship studies) and potent (IQ gains) at the same time?

Jensen (1973a, 1973b) made the paradox all the more acute by using a mathematical model. He plugged in two pieces of data: a 15-point IQ difference between two groups; and a low estimate of the influence of environment on IQ (a correlation between environment and IQ of about 0.33). These implied that for environment to explain the IQ gap between those groups, the environmental gap between them would have to be immense. One group would have to have an average environment so bad as to be worse than 99 percent of the environments among the other group. Dutch males of 1982 were 20 IQ points above the previous generation. According to Jensen's mathematics, the average environment of the previous generation would have to be worse than 99.99 percent of the 1982 environments. Jensen assumed that no one could make a case for something apparently so implausible.

Lewontin (1976a, 1976b) tried to solve the paradox. He distinguished the role of genes within groups from the role of genes between groups. He imagined a sack of seedcorn with plenty of genetic variation randomly divided into two batches, each of which would therefore be equal for overall genetic quality. Batch A is grown in a uniform and optimal environment, so within that group all height differences at maturity are due to genetic variation; batch B is grown in a uniform environment which lacks enough nitrates, so within that group all height differences are also genetic. However, the difference in average height between the two groups will, of course, be due entirely to the unequal quality of their two environments.

So now we seemed to have a solution. The present generation has some potent environmental advantage absent from the last generation that explains its higher average IQ. Let us call it Factor X. Factor X will simply not register in twin studies. After all, the two members of a twin pair are by definition of the same generation. Since Factor X was completely missing within the last generation, no one benefited from it at all and, therefore, it can hardly explain any IQ differences within the last generation. It will not dilute the dominance of genes. Since Factor X is completely uniform within the present generation, everyone benefits from it to the same degree and it cannot explain IQ differences within the present generation. Once again, the dominance of genes will be unchallenged. Therefore, twin studies could show that genes explain 100 percent of IQ differences within generations, and yet, environment might explain 100 percent of the average IQ difference between generations.

However, Lewontin offers us a poisoned apple. History has not experimented with the last two generations as we might experiment with plants in a laboratory. Consider the kind of factors that might explain massive IQ gains, such as better nutrition,

more education, more liberal parenting, and the slow spread of the
scientific ethos. It is quite unreal to imagine any of these affecting
two generations with uniformity. Certainly, everyone was not
badly nourished in the last generation, everyone well nourished
at present; everyone without secondary school in the last generation, everyone a graduate at present; everyone raised tradition-
ally in the last generation, everyone raised liberally at present;
everyone bereft of the scientific ethos in the last generation, everyone permeated with it at present. If the only solution to our paradox is to posit a Factor X or a collection of such, it seems even more
baffling than before. We should shut this particular door as follows: a solution is plausible only if it does not posit a Factor X.

Seven years ago, William Dickens of the Brookings
Institution decided to do some modeling of his own and asked
my help in applying it to real-world situations (Dickens & Flynn,
2001a, 2001b). We believe that it solves the identical twins paradox
without positing a Factor X. It makes an assumption that may seem
commonplace but which has profound implications, namely, that
those who have an advantage for a particular trait will become
matched with superior environments for that trait.

Recall studies of identical twins separated at birth and
reared by different families. When they grow up, they are very
similar and this is supposed to be due solely to the fact that they
have identical genes. But for that to be true, they must not be
atypically similar in environment; indeed, the assumption is that
they have no more environment in common than randomly
selected individuals. To show how unlikely this is, let us look at
the life history of a pair of identical twins.

John and Joe are separated at birth. Both live in an area (a
place like the state of Indiana) that is basketball-mad. Their identical genes make them both taller and quicker than average to the
same degree. John goes to school in one city, plays basketball a bit
better on the playground, enjoys it more, practices more than
most, catches the eye of the grade-school coach, plays on a team,

goes on to play in high school where he gets really professional coaching. Joe goes to school in a city a hundred miles away. However, precisely because his genes are identical to John's, precisely because he is taller and quicker than average to exactly the same degree, he is likely to have a very similar life history. After all, this is an area in which no talent for basketball is likely to go unnoticed.

On the other hand, Mark and Allen have identical genes that make them both a bit shorter and stodgier than average. They too are separated and go to different schools. However, they too have similar basketball life histories except, in their case, both play very little, develop few skills, and become mainly spectators.

In other words, genetic advantages that may have been quite modest at birth have a huge effect on eventual basketball skills by getting matched with better environments – and genes thereby get credit for the potency of powerful environmental factors, such as more practice, team play, professional coaching. It is not difficult to apply the analogy to IQ. One child is born with a slightly better brain than another. Which of them will tend to like school, be encouraged, start haunting the library, get into top-stream classes, and attend university? And if that child has a separated identical twin that has much the same academic history, what will account for their similar adult IQs? Not identical genes alone – the ability of those identical genes to co-opt environments of similar quality will be the missing piece of the puzzle.

Note that genes have profited from seizing control of a powerful instrument that multiplies causal potency, namely, feedback loops that operate between performance and its environment. A gene-caused performance advantage causes a more-homework-done environment, the latter magnifies the academic performance advantage, which upgrades the environment further by entry into a top stream, which magnifies the performance advantage once again, which gets access to a good university environment. Since these feedback loops so much influence the fate of individuals throughout their life histories, the Dickens/Flynn model calls them "individual multipliers."

Understanding how genes gain dominance over environment in kinship studies provides the key to how environment emerges with huge potency between generations. There must be persistent environmental factors that bridge the generations; and those factors must seize control of a powerful instrument that multiplies their causal potency.

The industrial revolution has persisted for 200 years and it affects every aspect of our lives. For example, look at what the industrial revolution did to basketball by the invention of TV. It gave basketball a mass audience and it increased the pay a professional player could expect. Basketball also had the advantage that ghetto blacks without access to playing fields could play it on a small concrete court. Wider and keener participation raised the general skill level: you had to shoot more and more accurately to excel. That higher average performance fed back into play: those who learned to shoot with either hand became the best – and then they became the norm – which meant you had to be able to pass with either hand to excel – and then that became the norm – and so forth. Every escalation of the average population performance raised individual performance, which escalated the average performance further, and you get a huge escalation of basketball skills in a single generation.

The advent of TV set into motion a new set of feedback loops that revolutionized the game. To distinguish these society-driven feedback loops from those gene-driven feedback loops that favor one individual over another, Dickens and Flynn call them "the social multiplier." Its essence is that rising average performance becomes a potent causal factor in its own right. The concept applies equally well to IQ gains over time.

The industrial revolution is both the child of the scientific revolution and the parent of the spread of the scientific worldview. It has changed every aspect of our lives. It demands and rewards additional years of education. When a grade-school education became the norm, everyone with middle-class aspirations wanted a high-school diploma. When their efforts made a high-school diploma the norm, everyone began to want a B.A. Economic progress creates new expectations about parents stimulating children, highly paid professional jobs in which we are expected to think for ourselves, more cognitively demanding leisure activities. No one wants to seem deficient as a parent, unsuited for promotion, boring as a companion. Everyone responds to the new milieu by enhancing their performance, which pushes the average higher, so they respond to that new average, which pushes the average higher still. You get a huge escalation of cognitive skills in a single generation.

So now, everything is clear. Within a generation, genetic differences drive feedback processes – genes use individual multipliers to determine and magnify IQ differences between individuals. Between generations, environmental trends drive feedback processes – environment uses social multipliers to raise the average IQ over time. Twin studies, despite their evidence for feeble environmental factors, and IQ trends over time, despite their revelation of potent environmental factors, present no paradox. What dominates depends on what seizes control of powerful multipliers. Without the concept of multipliers, all is confusion. There is nothing more certain than this. If twin studies of basketball were done, they would show the separated twins growing up with very similar skills. And Jensen's mathematics would "show" that environment was far too weak to cause massive gains in basketball performance over time. Which is to say we would demonstrate the impossibility of what we know to be true.

Best of all, our solution posits no Factor X. Nothing said assumes that social changes from one time to another were uniform in their impact on individuals. Better education, better parent–child relationships, better work, better leisure, all may raise the quality of the range of environments available from one generation to another. But the magnitude of the differences between quality of environments from best to worse can remain the same. Genetic differences between individuals can continue to match people with better or worse environments to the same degree they always did. Even though slam dunks and passing behind the back become common, being tall and quick will still co-opt a better basketball environment. Even though people in general get better at solving intellectually demanding problems, being born with a bit better brain will still co-opt a better than average school environment. In a word, the operation of social multipliers over time does not abolish the operation of individual multipliers in the life histories of individuals.

IQ gains and the real world

At one time, I was blind to the real-world significance of IQ gains because I was under the spell of g. I kept looking for general intelligence gains and could not find them. I could not see the trees because I was looking for a forest.

Eventually, I came to see that piecemeal gains do not lose their real-world significance simply because there are not gains everywhere. Indeed, if trends that show no gains are significant, it follows logically that trends that do show gains are significant. If failure to make progress on the Vocabulary and Information subtests of the WISC illuminates why high-school seniors are no better at reading serious literature, then huge gains on Raven's and Similarities must mean something. Why should some subtests of the WISC have real-world significance and not others?

I think that I have made a strong case that IQ gains show an enhanced real-world capacity to view the world through scientific spectacles. I believe I can show that this has enormous potential to alter human cognition. Take that claim as a promissory note that I will redeem in Chapter 7. IQ gains also show that we can attack abstract and visual-symbolic problems more successfully and that we are better at on-the-spot problem solving on tasks removed from concrete reality. The concept of reciprocal causality is liberating in this context: if an activity causes a rise in a cognitive skill, then that enhanced cognitive skill must be a prerequisite for performing that activity.

Schooler shows (1998) that professional work roles enhance our ability to be innovative. They could hardly do that unless innovation was necessary to perform professional duties; and since society needs more and more people to do managerial and technical and professional jobs, gains in the ability to think on the spot rather than just following a rule book have social significance. A study by Leong, Hartung, Goh, and Gaylor (2001) suggests that first-born children tend to have more cognitive and analytic interests, while later-borns are more artistic and oriented to the outdoors. Since middle-class mores and aspirations have reduced family size, a higher percentage of children are first-born and are going to have more cognitive and analytic interests. If that is so, enhanced cognitive skills become a prerequisite for performing like a good parent. Parents will have to take their children's "hypothetical" questions seriously, that is, answer rather than dismiss the eternal string of "whys" to which children are prone.

Then there is the world of leisure. Greenfield (1998) argues that video games, popular electronic games, and computer applications cause enhanced problem solving in visual and symbolic contexts; if that is so, that kind of enhanced problem solving is necessary if we are to fully enjoy our leisure. Johnson (2005) points to the cognitive demands of video games, for example, the spatial geometry of Tetris, the engineering riddles of Myst, and the mapping of Grand Theft Auto.

However, Johnson's most important contribution is his analysis of television. TV aims at a mass audience and, therefore, its level of cognitive complexity is based on an estimate of what the average person can assimilate. Johnson shows convincingly that today's popular TV programs make unprecedented cognitive demands. The popular shows of a generation ago, such as *I love Lucy* and *Dragnet* and *Starsky and Hutch*, were simplistic requiring virtually no concentration to follow. Beginning in 1981 with *Hill Street Blues*, single-episode drama began to be replaced with dramas that wove together as many as ten threads into the plot line. A recent episode of the hit drama *24* connected the lives of twenty-one characters, each with a distinct story.

Howard (1999) uses traditional games as an informal measure of cognitive gains. He anticipated the potency of the social multiplier. He speaks of "cascading feed-back loops": more people want to play chess, the average skill rises, chess clubs form, coaching and chess books improve with rising demand, so you have even better average performance, and so on. He evidences the trend toward enhanced skills by documenting the decline in the age of chess grandmasters. There is no doubt that the standard of play in chess tournaments has risen (Nunn, 1999). Howard makes the same case, although the evidence is less compelling, for feedback loops in other leisure activities that are cognitively demanding such as playing bridge and Go.

Remembering numbers

This account of factors that are good candidates for the role of cause in explaining IQ trends over time is by no means exhaustive. There are other cognitive skills I did not intend to include because my hypotheses as to causes are purely speculative rather than semi-speculative. Nonetheless, I will now discuss them.

We have little on memory trends over time. Until recently, the Digit Span subtest was not one of the ten core subtests of the WISC, but what data exist show almost no gain from 1972 to 2002 (see Appendix I, Table 1). This test measures not only rote memory but also working memory. After digits are read out in a random order, subjects repeat as many as they can (Digit Span forward); after another series is read out, subjects try to put as many as they can in reverse order (Digit Span backward). Perhaps society has not improved this cognitive skill because we need no greater store of memories and no greater ability to reorder memories when we deal with the world today than we did thirty years ago. Memory is such a fundamental asset I see no reason why it should not have been at a high level a century ago. A society could reorder its priorities in a strange way, of course, and give immense prizes for feats of memory.

But note that Digit Span has to do with memory of numbers and that kind of memory may be a law unto itself. Even in 1900, there were telephone numbers and street addresses and numbered playing cards, so the demands made on number memory may have been constant over the past century. Hoosain (1991) makes one wonder if there is not some quasi-physiological limit on number memory that bridges time and space. For example, Chinese children do better on Digit Span forward than English children. Hoosain found that this was entirely a matter of how many digits you could say at normal speed in a given time in the two languages. The pronunciation of the number words for one to nine in Chinese takes on average about 80 percent of the time it does in English. And English children remember only 80 percent as many digits after they have been read out. In other words, both races can remember as many numbers as the examiner reads out over the same period of time, that is, about two or three seconds (see Box 5).

Even more impressive, children fluent in both English and Chinese do only 80 percent as well when given Digit Span in English as they do when it is administered in Chinese. This issues a warning to those who make cross-cultural comparisons without making a functional analysis of what is going on. This admonition will take on added significance when we come to elementary cognitive tasks such as Reaction Times.

Two WISC subtests are designed to measure the speed with which we can process information. Coding and Symbol Search

---

Box 5

Hoosain (1991, pp. 64–66) presents preliminary data which show that the time span for recalling numbers is similar for English, Welsh, Chinese, Spanish, Hebrew, and Arabic. He presents better data for three dialects of Chinese and English. Note that the ratio of numbers recalled virtually matches the ratio between the number of English number words and the number of Chinese number words that it is normal to read out per unit time. In other words, fewer English number words are read out per second and English subjects recall fewer words after they are read out:

English/Cantonese:	0.844 (time)	— (DS forward)	—
English/Mandarin:	0.770 (time)	0.783 (DS forward)	adult
English/Putonghua:	0.800 (time)	0.854 (DS forward)	ages 4–6

---

made substantial gains equivalent to 4.75 IQ points in the brief period from 1989 to 2002 (see Appendix I, Table 1). Symbol Search became a core subtest only recently and, therefore, the supporting data are less extensive than in the case of Coding. Perhaps the speeded-up tempo of events on visual media like TV is conditioning people and, therefore, having some effect on the speed with which they can absorb information.

From solutions to new problems

Whatever explanations we offer for cognitive trends over time, we must not allow factor analysis to make us think about intelligence in a way we would find odd in any other area. The fact that good people tend to be both generous and tolerant would not blind us to the significance of trends that pick and choose from among the virtues. Thanks to declining racial bias over time, the present generation might be more tolerant and yet, thanks to no decline in materialism, no more generous. America would still be a better place for blacks. The fact that musical people tend to be superior at both the piano and the drums would not blind us to trends that favor one instrument over another. Thanks to more interest in pop music, the standard of drumming might rise and thanks to no more interest in classical music, piano expertise might not increase. America would still be a better place for those who like pop music.

Fortunately, there is in fact enough interest in classical music among an elite to motivate those who play to improve their skills. But there is no reason to think that performances on various instruments are being enhanced in accord with their g loadings.

This chapter is my best shot at resolving the paradoxes that have bedeviled the phenomenon of massive IQ gains over time. If my solutions are correct, they imply a new approach to the study of human intelligence. The best way to introduce that approach is to present a critique of a current theory of intelligence based on something by now familiar: the concept of g.

3 Towards a new theory of intelligence

> We cannot avoid the problems raised by the concept of a uni-
> versal good. Naturally, we are reluctant because it was invented
> by friends of ours, but for a philosopher ... an even better
> friend must be the truth.
>
> (Aristotle, *Ethics*, i, 6, 1096a, 11–16)

Theory is not as exciting as trying to capture the thinking of our
ancestors. General readers may find that this chapter takes some
pondering. I believe it is worth the effort. Among other things, it
gives my views on what will advance our knowledge of intelligence. There is a section on how a chimpanzee defeats humans
on an important cognitive task. Have faith: later on we will be
discussing things like how people can enhance their mental abilities (the advice is pretty common sense but worth taking), the fate
of convicts on death row, and whether we can achieve the wisdom
needed to cope with the problems of the twenty-first century.

I am going to stress the limitations of g but feel a certain
reluctance to do so. Arthur Jensen has done brilliant work in
exploiting its potential, and virtually everything I have done in
psychology has been a response to problems and challenges posed
by Jensen. His theory has a great beauty rather like that of Plato's
theory of Forms. But I am now convinced that we must transcend a
g-ocentric approach to make further progress.

The difficulty with g is dual. It confuses the problem of
providing a definition of intelligence because any attempt at a
definition looks pallid by comparison. Moreover, its natural

kingdom is the level of individual differences and its adherents tend to treat the social and physiological dimensions of intelligence as territory to be explored mainly because they might enhance the significance of *g*. I believe we need a BIDS approach to intelligence: one that treats the brain, individual differences, and social trends as having equal integrity and attempts to integrate what they tell us into a coherent whole. The three levels are interrelated and each has the right to propose hypotheses about what ought to happen on another level.

That said, I will undertake the following tasks:

(1) Solve the problem of defining intelligence.
(2) Introduce the BIDS approach: its three levels and their dominant concepts.
(3) Defend the integrity of the three levels against conceptual imperialism.
(4) Give some examples of cross-fertilization between the levels.
(5) Assess whether *g* poses interesting hypotheses on the brain physiology level.
(6) Assess proposals to supplement *g* with other constructs on the individual differences level.
(7) Give some advice to those who design IQ tests.

Intelligence and celestial influence

Jensen (1972, p. 76) wrote one passage in which he said that "intelligence, by definition, is what intelligence tests measure." This is called instrumentalism, or defining what you are trying to measure by referring to the readings of the measuring instrument, and it is subject to devastating critique. If intelligence is what current IQ tests measure, we could never invent a better IQ test because the new test, by definition, would be a departure from what measures intelligence.

Actually, Jensen was never that naive. In 1979, he wrote a brilliant paper distinguishing intelligence from both learning and memory. He imagined Robinson Crusoe alone on his island struggling to survive. Crusoe would forget things and, therefore, have the concept of memory. He would acquire new skills and, therefore, have the concept of learning. However, it would only be when his man Friday arrived and learned those skills faster and better than he had learned them that he would develop the concept of intelligence (Jensen, 1979).

Unfortunately, some eight years ago, Jensen (1998) abandoned this start toward a definition of intelligence in favor of vowing never to use the word. He had become disgusted with intelligence: it had no precision and attracted no consensus. It could not measure up to the scientific construct called g: the latter was precise, measurable, and enormously fruitful.

Jensen did not, of course, stick to his resolve. He reports Garber's attempt to multiply intelligences by pinning the word on tests of musical ability, body-kinesthetic skills, and personal skills. As Jensen says, this sort of thing is no more sensible than calling chess an athletic skill. But why is that so: one pushes the pieces across the board? It is because when the chips are down, he introduces a distinction between "mental abilities" and "physical abilities" (Jensen, 1998, pp. 52–53). On occasion he lapses into his old wording. For example he says that "intelligence" predicts the rate and quality and limits of learning (Jensen, 1998, pp. 274–275). The inverted commas surrounding the word do not disguise the fact that he has had to use it. He even uses a substitute for the Robinson Crusoe scenario: someone who learns darts faster and better has more aptitude than someone who learns it slowly and poorly (Jensen, 1998, p. 95).

Any attempt to avoid defining intelligence is bad faith. The only reason we can dispense with a clarified concept is that we all have an unclarified concept in mind. Imagine that Jensen presented a lecture on g to a Martian and never did use some viable substitute for the word "intelligence." The Martian would ask in bewilderment, but what kind of a theory is this, is it perhaps a theory of the tides? When Jensen answered, of course not, it was a theory abut measuring who learns best and fastest, the Martian would exclaim: "Oh, you mean it is a theory of intelligence."

Endless muddling about the definition of intelligence is a distraction from getting on with the job of theory construction, so in a sense Jensen's instincts were sound, but the distraction is not going to go away until it is exorcized. The best start is to note Jensen's reason for abandoning the definitional task: all definitions of intelligence compare badly with the theoretical construct of g. I will argue that the roles of a pre-theory concept and a post-theory concept are quite different and that to confuse the two is fatal. The best example comes from the history of astronomy. It tells us how the modern pre-theory concept of celestial influence paved the way for the post-theory concepts of whirlpool, gravity, and space warping.

Aristotle bequeathed to the West a pre-theory concept of celestial influence we have now abandoned. That was because it gave bad advice to astronomical theories. It assumed that heavenly bodies were "guided" into certain orbits. This engendered a certain theory. That the Gods loved beauty, that circles were the most beautiful curve, and that the Gods "pushed" heavenly bodies into circular orbits. Therefore, theory should try to reduce the motions of heavenly bodies to circles. Other theories were possible. A skeptic might want to dispense with the Gods and posit that forces within planets (like what causes volcanic eruptions) pushed them through the heavens in a programmed orbit, rather like a guided missile. This would have had the advantage of leaving open whether orbits were circles or some other kind of curve, but the dominance of Ptolemy's theory of circular motion meant that other possibilities went unrealized.

In early modern times, there arose a new pre-theory concept of celestial influence that gave different advice. It posited that the size and propinquity of heavenly bodies to one another might well influence their motions; and noted the central role this would give the Sun in the solar system. This engendered a number of theories. Descartes (without evidence) posited that the Sun rotated on its axis and created a whirlpool that swung the planets around their orbits. In other words, he gave the pre-theory concept greater specificity by developing it into a theory-embedded concept; indeed, he gave it the measurability needed to generate precise predictions. These were falsified. The trouble could have been with the pre-theory concept (bad advice) or the peculiar nature of the theory (wrong mechanics and mathematics).

Newton showed that it was the latter by supplying a better post-theory concept based on the same pre-theory concept. He abandoned a whirlpool in favor of gravity. By assuming that bodies attracted one another proportionately to mass and inversely to distance squared, his theory gave a wonderful range of non-falsified predictions. Then a few began to go astray, for example, telescopes showed Mercury's actual orbit did not exactly match the predicted orbit. Einstein gave us an even better post-theory concept, one still based on the same pre-theory concept of celestial influence. He abandoned gravity in favor of the propensity of space–time to curve in the vicinity of mass. The Sun creates a funnel; and Mercury spins around it with its orbit determined by the curvature of the funnel at its location.

What can we learn from this? First, pre-theory concepts are not useless. They give good or bad advice about the direction theory formation should take. They can be assumed without being stated, witness the later Jensen, and if a good one is assumed in sufficient detail, little harm is done – except for the likelihood of endless debate about defining intelligence. Second, they must strike a balance; they should be specific enough to offer advice but general enough to let theory do its job. It is up to theory to embed the pre-theory concept into a theoretical structure and give it the specificity to engender predictions precise enough to be falsified. It is hardly odd that when Jensen compared the pre-theory concept of intelligence with the theory-embedded construct of g, he found the former wanting. He wanted the concept of intelligence to do the impossible: accomplish what only a theory can do.

I will now offer a pre-theory concept of intelligence. It consists of an answer to a question: what traits affect our ability to solve problems with cognitive content?

(1) Mental acuity: the ability to provide on-the-spot solutions to problems we have never encountered before, problems not solvable by mechanical application of a learned method, and often requiring us to create alternative solutions from which we must choose.

(2) Habits of mind: the rise of science engendered new habits of mind of enormous potency. It detached logic and the hypothetical from the concrete and today we use them to attack a whole range of new problems. A more mundane example: ten years ago, I began to do crossword puzzles. I now do them much better, not because of increased mental acuity or even larger vocabulary or store of information. My usual proclivity with words is to use them to say what I want as simply and directly as possible. I had to modify that habit to imagine secondary meanings, less literal meanings, reflect whether the clue word was being "used" as a noun or a verb, and so forth.

(3) Attitudes: these lay the foundation for acquiring habits of mind. We had to learn to take the taxonomy of science seriously before we could put on the scientific spectacles through which we now view the world. We have to take abstract problem solving seriously before we will do much of it in our leisure and be adept at it as we enter the test room.

(4) Knowledge and information: the more you have, the more problems you can attack. You cannot do advanced algebra

without knowing elementary algebra. You cannot put knowledge to work without data.

(5) Speed of information processing, whereby one assimilates new data and the quicker the better if problems must be solved within time limits.

(6) Memory, whereby one accesses knowledge and information.

When we speak of intelligence, we sometimes adopt a narrow usage that focuses on mental acuity, as when we say someone is intelligent, even though they are mentally lazy, or ignorant, or uninformed, or slow, or have a poor memory. The broad usage refers to all of the above, all of the cognitive traits, habits of mind, contents of the mind, and attitudes that direct the investment of mental energy and make us good solvers of cognitively demanding problems. Clearly there are many other traits that contribute to cognitive problem solving, for example, physical states like being healthy, not being deaf, being conscious, and so forth. But to state everything relevant would be never-ending because it would encompass the entire universe (living on a planet capable of sustaining life).

I think the above definition strikes the right balance. It is broad enough to allow for cross-cultural variation. Different societies have different values and attitudes that determine what cognitive problems are worth the investment of mental energy. It is also broad enough to allow for all present alternative theories.

The debates about whether a theory that embeds intelligence in the form of g is adequate, or whether g should give way to a triple concept of analytic-practical-creative intelligence à la Sternberg, or be supplemented by "emotional intelligence" à la Goleman, are all embodiments of the same pre-theory concept. Sternberg argues that measurement of what I have called mental acuity is incomplete unless it extends to the ability to devise on-the-spot solutions to real-life problems and the sort of creativity that shows a fertile imagination. Goleman argues that character traits like empathy deserve more emphasis because they greatly expand the range of problems we can attack.

Is the above definition narrow enough to offer good advice to those who want to make intelligence measurable and specific? I believe the record shows that, whether consciously or not, those who developed the major IQ tests had something like it in mind and took its advice.

Raven's Progressive Matrices tries to isolate mental acuity or intelligence narrow as much as possible from the other components of intelligence broad. It does this by demanding that the examinee solve cognitively demanding problems on the spot that require a minimum of learned method, knowledge, and information. It is supposed to be administered untimed to minimize the role of speed of information processing and spatial memory of matrices designs. However, it cannot avoid measuring habits of mind. Note that after people shifted from reasoning on the concrete to the formal level, Raven's scores began to rise dramatically.

As for WISC subtests, Similarities, Block Design, Object Assembly, Picture Arrangement, and Picture Completion all measure mental acuity to some degree. Information and Vocabulary measure what they say. Arithmetic measures learning what schools teach as mathematics. Comprehension measures understanding the mechanics of everyday life. Coding and Symbol Search measure processing speed. Forward Digit Span isolates memory from the other components of intelligence broad. My classification of subtests differs from that offered in the WISC manuals (Wechsler, 1992, pp. 2, 7, and 187). Theirs is based on factor analysis, mine on matching test content with functional mental processes.

I have no illusion that this solution to the problem of defining intelligence will end debate. But it may do so among those who really wish to get on with the task of theory construction.

Three levels and three concepts

Intelligence is important on three levels, namely, brain physiology, individual differences, and social trends. The core of a BIDS approach to intelligence is that each of those levels has its own organizing concept and it is a mistake to impose the architectonic concept of one level on another. I want to stress that the mere notion of three levels adds nothing to our knowledge of intelligence. What it does is clarify what kind of research might lead to greater knowledge. It is not itself a theory in the sense of making sense of what we observe. It stands between our pre-theory concept of intelligence and genuine theory, which is to say that it is an additional piece of advice. The rest of this chapter is a defense of its probity.

The best analogy I can find from the history of science is the controversy between Huygens, who championed the wave theory of light, and Newton, who held it was a stream of corpuscles (particles). Much time was wasted before it was realized that light could act like a wave in certain of its manifestations and like a steam of particles in other manifestations. We have to realize that intelligence can act like a highly correlated set of abilities on one level and like a set of functionally independent abilities on other levels.

The levels and their organizing concepts:

(1) The brain. Highly localized neural clusters are developed differentially as a result of specialized cognitive exercise. There are also important factors that affect all neural clusters such as blood supply, dopamine as a substance that render synapses receptive to registering experience, and the input of the stress-response system. For the present, I think it important to emphasize specialization over commonality and will call the brain's organizing concept "neural decentralization."

(2) Individual differences. Performance differences between individuals on a wide variety of cognitive tasks are correlated primarily in terms of the cognitive complexity of the task (fluid g), or the posited cognitive complexity of the path toward mastery (crystallized g). Information may not seem to differentiate individuals for intelligence but if two people have the same opportunity, the better mind is likely to accumulate a wider range of information. I will call this concept "general intelligence" or g.

(3) Society. Various real-world cognitive skills show different trends over time as a result of shifting social priorities. I will call this concept "social utility."

We are a long way from integrating what is known on these three levels into one body of theory. The best strategy is to use them to cross-fertilize one another, that is, use one level to pose hypotheses on another level. This is worthwhile in itself but it can also lead to a piece of luck, namely, a paradox. It may seem odd to describe a paradox as lucky, but it is through resolving paradoxes that we are likely to take steps toward integrating the three levels. However, when we cross from one level to another, there is a temptation to be avoided, namely, conceptual imperialism.

Conceptual imperialism

Assume that we are cross-fertilizing between levels. We use one level to pose a hypothesis on another and want to test that hypothesis. Conceptual imperialism has an explicit and implicit form. The explicit form is using the organizing concept of the "donor" level to assess the truth of the hypothesis on the "recipient" level. The implicit form is simply ignoring the organizing concept of the recipient level in testing the hypothesis. Our struggle to solve our paradoxes affords some good examples because part of the solution was to shake off the effects of conceptual imperialism.

Our first paradox arose when we took a result from the individual differences level, that various cognitive abilities were highly correlated, and used it to pose a hypothesis on the social level: if cognitive gains over time are significant, gains on a variety of abilities ought to mimic their factor loadings. If they do not, if they are at variance with their g loadings (and with other factor loadings), they must be "hollow." Jensen (1998, p. 332) uses this term. He believes that if IQ gains are caused by social rather than biological factors, they are non-g gains with little real-world significance, that is, they signal no enhancement of important problem-solving abilities. At best, they might signal enhancement of narrow tasks that are highly test specific. In other words, Jensen makes no attempt to assess subtest gains in terms of social utility. Rather than using the organizing concept of the social level to assess trends on that level, he drags the concept of g across from the individual differences level and assigns it a job for which it is unsuited.

Here I will simply remind the reader of all you miss if you are blinded by g and factor analysis. Factor analysis yields no factor called "looking at the world through scientific spectacles" or "freeing logic and the hypothetical from the concrete." Yet these have great social significance. Failure to develop larger everyday vocabularies and funds of information may be "hollow" and test specific but they affect our ability to interpret and enjoy adult literature. Indeed, rather than being narrow in their impact, they affect virtually everything that makes us human. What a pity that they do not get the blessing of factor analysis. Then we would know that they really were significant.

Our fourth paradox took another finding from the individual differences level, that twin studies show genes to be far more potent than environment in explaining individual differences in IQ, and posed a hypothesis on the social level: if society has not enhanced the genetic quality of its population over time, real cognitive skill gains must be minimal. Here the cultural imperialism is implicit rather than explicit. The heritability of g dominates the search for the causes of IQ gains: they just must be the result of something like hybrid vigor (which upgrades genes) or nutrition (which at least upgrades brain physiology directly). And when something like the Dickens/Flynn model suggests that exogenous environmental factors have affected social priorities (have triggered social multipliers of various cognitive abilities), it is greeted with great suspicion. The suspicion is based on an unstated assumption: that the social level simply ought to dance to the tune of the individual differences level rather than have its own rhythm.

Note that the emergence of these two paradoxes was lucky in the sense that their solutions necessitated models that integrated the individual differences and social levels. My "decathlon model" is a crude attempt to show how various abilities that are correlated on the individual differences level (sprints and high jump) can be functionally distinct on the social level (you can have progress in the sprints and none in the high jump). The Dickens/Flynn "basketball model" has been given mathematical precision but performs the same kind of integrative function. It shows just how genetically dominated cognitive differences on the individual differences level turn into environmentally driven trends on the social level.

Also note that the fact that these hypotheses originated on the individual differences level is a historical phenomenon. Our knowledge of what happens on the individual differences level began to accumulate a century ago, while real knowledge of cognitive trends over time began about twenty-five years ago. If the latter had antedated the former, the hypotheses would have run in the other direction: how can environment be so feeble on the individual differences level; how can performance differences be so highly correlated on the individual differences level?

The question of whether g has a physiological substratum is still to be determined but I suspect it does, albeit the depth of that substratum may be exaggerated. However, this gives the concept of g no right to conceptual imperialism, that is, g has no right to assess evidence of what happens in brain physiology. As we shall see, skills swimming freely of g also have a physiological substratum. Their degree of autonomy there may be far greater on the brain level than that normally present on the level of individual differences.

I suspect that g poses less of a threat of cognitive imperialism on the brain level than on the social level. On the social level, there is the temptation to classify the unwelcome evidence of IQ gains over time as an artifact due to test sophistication or cultural bias. It is hard to imagine anyone using those labels to dismiss physiological evidence. Therefore, it may be said that I am ringing a false alarm. Very well: but surely there is no harm in locking a room that no reasonable person would want to enter. By way of excuse, when Blair (2006) put forward his evidence of the autonomy of various cognitive skills on the brain level, he received some scholarly correspondence that revealed g-ocentric tendencies.

Closing a door to conceptual imperialism

There is one door ajar that conceptual imperialism might sneak through. We have seen that IQ gains over time are not factor invariant, which is to say that gains on the various WISC subtests do not match their factor loadings and, most important, do not match their g loadings. It may seem self-evident that, whatever social significance various skill gains over time may have, they cannot be g gains. And yet, Dickens and Flynn (2006) have shown that this is not so: black Americans gained 5.5 IQ points on white Americans between 1972 and 2002; the gains were not factor invariant; and yet the g gap between black and white Americans closed by the equivalent of 5.13 points. How is that possible?

The simplest answer is that if one group really could not make g gains on another, they would be incapable of making gains on cognitive tasks that have heavy g loadings. We have already seen that the present generation has made huge gains compared to the last on Raven's, perhaps the test with the highest g loading of them all. There is no evidence that the test was drained of its normal cognitive complexity by being taught and the items thereby reduced to a measure of rote memory. There is no evidence that the gains are a matter of growing test sophistication or cultural bias. Therefore, if a group can make gains on a test like Raven's, and all of the WISC subtests that are heavily g loaded, the group is capable of making g gains. The mere fact that the pattern of gains does not correlate with the differential g loadings of the subtests will not make the gains go away – unless you are tempted by conceptual imperialism and say that the gains just cannot be gains in terms of cognitive complexity.

We should keep in mind why g has a claim to be a theory-embedded concept of intelligence. The greater the g loading, the greater the cognitive complexity of the task: making a soufflé has a higher g loading than scrambling eggs. If it were the reverse, if g rose to the extent a task was simple and automatic, we would dismiss it as an index of regurgitation of memorized material or skills. Now imagine that score gains on all of the WISC subtests were three times as great as they are. They would still have the same pattern, that is, they would still flunk the test of factor invariance and not qualify as g gains against that criterion. But could we dismiss the enhancement of performance on so many cognitively complex tasks? Whatever factor analysis might say, they would have captured the essence of g.

If the above analysis holds true for the gains of one generation compared to another, it can hold true for black gains on white. However, to avoid reception of the approach to intelligence presented herein being derailed by those who care only about race and IQ – look what happened to the Bell Curve – I shall shift from a racial example to one less likely to arouse strong emotion. Imagine there were two groups genetically equal in their potential for hearing:

(1) Group A has a less favorable environment than Group B because far more of them work in factories where the noise level damages hearing. It damages it more as you go from low to high-pitched sounds.

(2) We have a hearing test with four subtests: traffic noise, alarm clocks, conversation, and music. Each has a different pitch loading running from lower to higher in the order listed.

(3) The hearing aid is invented. Group A benefits disproportionately because, of course, more of them suffer from hearing loss and try to get one. However, the hearing aids are not quite as good at allowing you to pick up high-pitched sounds.

(4) Weighting the four subtests equally gives HQ (hearing quotient). Thanks to hearing aids, Group A has made up 5.5 points (SD = 15) of its hearing deficit on Group B. However, subtest by subtest, its gains are very slightly in reverse order in terms of pitch loadings. Therefore, they do not match the pitch hierarchy and are not pitch invariant.

(5) We weight the various subtests in terms of their pitch loadings (music gets more weight than traffic noise) and derive a PQ (pitch quotient).

(6) This shows that Group A has made up 5.13 points on Group B in terms of PQ, almost as much as it did in terms of HQ.

Well, there is nothing mysterious about this. Group A made big gains on Group B on all four subtests. The gains run counter to the pitch loadings but this is mitigated by two factors: the pitch differentials between the subtests are small; the discrimination against high pitch by the hearing aids is also small. Therefore, when the gains are converted from HQ to PQ by weighting the subtests, the fact that the gains were not factor invariant makes little difference: "anti-pitch" gains convert into pitch gains that are almost as large as the hearing gains. This scenario implies that to reach pitch quotient parity, Group A would have to attain a small hearing quotient advantage. It is unlikely that hearings aids would ever do this because they would have to somehow favor Group A: they would have to allow Group A to hear high-pitched sounds as well as Group B and low-pitched sounds better.

Hearing aids have not addressed the root cause of the hearing gap. Group A are still disproportionately in factory work, something that damages hearing differentially in terms of pitch. The only way to address the root cause would be to close the occupational gap between the groups, so that they both had the same percentage in white-collar and blue-collar jobs. And that might happen: thanks to better hearing and getting more out of school, Group A might actually get more white-collar jobs. At last, the root cause would be addressed and the pitch gap would disappear without the need for HQ superiority.

Cross-fertilization between levels

I should made it clear that many hypotheses from the individual differences level to the social level pose no paradoxes and have proved fruitful. The Bell Curve uses the g-ocentric theory of individual differences to analysis social trends. Without endorsing that analysis wholesale – for example, I consider the meritocracy thesis to be incoherent (Flynn, 2000a) – some things are clearly true. If most of a group is below the IQ or g threshold needed to qualify for professional, managerial, or technical jobs, it is likely to have few of its members in those jobs. If high IQ engenders attitudes and assets that make marriage more attractive, high-IQ mothers are less likely to have illegitimate children than low-IQ mothers.

These predictions have to be qualified in the light of other social factors. When white and black women are matched for IQ, far more of the latter are still solo-mothers, so other potent social forces must be at work. Flynn and Dickens (under review) argue that a worse marriage market within the black community is one of the missing factors. As for occupational thresholds, Flynn (1991a) showed that thanks to peculiar character traits, Chinese Americans could overcome the usual IQ thresholds for professions to a surprising degree, that is, their occupational profile fosters the illusion of a group with a mean IQ far above their actual mean.

Thus far we have neglected the level of brain physiology. The Dickens/Flynn model assumes that the brain behaves much like our muscles. It assumes that current environment has large effects on cognitive skills and that those skills atrophy with disuse. That poses the hypothesis that brain physiology should show the beneficial effects of current cognitive exercise throughout life.

Cohen (2005) compares the brains of younger and older adults and notes that people are often in their early fifties before dendrites reach their greatest number and complexity. No matter what their age, people must not give up mental exercise. Andel *et al.* (2005) found that people engaged in cognitively complex occupations are protected to some extent against the risk of dementia and Alzheimer's. Melton (2005) describes the dramatic case of Richard Wetherill. He played chess in retirement and could think eight moves ahead. In 2001, he was alarmed because he could only think four moves ahead and took a battery of tests designed to spot early dementia. He passed them all easily and continued an active mental life until his death in 2003. Autopsy showed that his brain was riddled with the plaques and tangles that are characteristic of Alzheimer's. Most people would have been reduced to a state of total confusion.

I do not wish to raise false hopes: note that Wetherill's high level of cognitive exercise did not keep his cognitive abilities from declining with age. The hypothesis posed by the Dickens/Flynn model can be made more explicit: the benefit from cognitive exercise will hold for all ages; and the benefit will not be lessened because the exercise regime is postponed until later life. This does not deny the fact that the aging brain causes everyone's performance to decline. The active mind will perform better than the inactive mind at 20; the former will still be much the same amount above the latter at 60; but both will decline in tandem from 20 to 60. Hold fast to the image of the brain as a muscle. At any age, an athlete is better off for training; but however hard you train, your times will get slower as you age (Salthouse, 2006).

Another cross-level hypothesis: social trends show that various cognitive skills are largely functionally independent of one another; therefore, the same must be true on the physiological level. If one neural area was developed in precisely the same way both when we do arithmetical reasoning exercise and when we do Raven's exercise, then progress on one would entail progress on the other.

This prompts a critical approach to MRI (magnetic resonance imaging) findings that the "same area" of the brain lights up when we do any kind of abstract reasoning. First, we cannot as yet distinguish between whether lighting up means that the area is being activated or whether it means that the area is being inhibited. Second, other physiological knowledge suggests that "areas" are too crude and miss highly specialized structures more subtle than areas. You use your arms and your legs when both swimming and running, but the two exercises have subtle effects on the muscles so that they do not reinforce one another. Before we can claim to know much, it looks as if we will actually need a "picture" of small clusters of neurons and the dendrites that connect them being strengthened by certain kinds of mental exercise. Even the science of sports physiology is not that far advanced on the neural level, that is, it cannot really give a differential picture of how the brain is behaving when we are running and hurdling.

The strictures of g do not apply on the brain level. If the emerging picture of brain physiology was that of an organ so structured that no one cognitive ability could be enhanced without enhancing others, then factor analysis and g would have stumbled on to the brain's organizational plan. As Clancy Blair (2006) shows, the brain is not like that (see Box 6). He took advantage of the fact that brain pathology provides experimental conditions no one could justify if provided by human intervention. Trauma, metabolic disorders, and unusual stress affect certain areas of the brain more than others. Blair found that subjects thus affected were not handicapped for all mental abilities, rather their brains were sufficiently decentralized so that they could pick and choose from the bundle of cognitive abilities wrapped up together by g. Damage to the pre-fontal cortex (see Figure 2) vetoed a normal level of on-the-spot problem-solving ability while, at the same time, undamaged areas fostered normal levels of other cognitive abilities. In other words, the brain can unravel g into its component parts.

It has long been known that certain neurons spray dopamine in the area surrounding them rather like a sprinkler. Any

---

Box 6

Blair (2006) summarizes his analysis of the physiological literature as follows:

> The association between fluid function and general intelligence is limited in ways that are important for understanding the development of cognitive competence ... The limits of the association between fluid cognition and general intelligence may be most pronounced in populations in which specific environmental and/or genetic background factors are distinct from those of normative or typically developing populations. These instances help to "pull apart" fluid cognition and g.

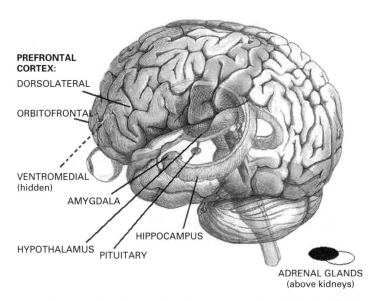

PREFRONTAL
CORTEX:
DORSOLATERAL

ORBITOFRONTAL

VENTROMEDIAL
(hidden)
          AMYGDALA

                HIPPOCAMPUS
HYPOTHALAMUS   PITUITARY

ADRENAL GLANDS
(above kidneys)

Figure 2 The prefrontal cortex is an area associated with fluid
cognition or on-the-spot problem solving. Blair found cases in which
there was damage to this area and, of course, fluid cognition was
impaired. But other skills like Information, Vocabulary, and
Comprehension were not. The hippocampus is associated with
spatial orientation. Maguire found it enlarged in the brains of taxi
drivers.

synapses in the vicinity that have recently been active, that is, have
had information passing across them, will react to the dopamine
and be strengthened. Strengthening a particular web of synapses
means that it will be easier in the future to fire off those neurons
and thus reproduce the same pattern of activity.

Maguire *et al.* (2000) found that the brains of London taxi
drivers were peculiar. They have an enlarged hippocampus (see
Figure 2) which is the brain area used for navigating three-
dimensional space. Here we see spatial abilities being developed
without comparable development of other cognitive skills. To
develop a wide variety of cognitive skills you need a wide variety
of exercise. It will be interesting when someone assesses the effects
of Kawashima's brain-training regime. A variety of mini-games

include solving simple math problems, counting people going in and out of a house, drawing pictures on the Nintendo DS touch screen, and reading classical literature aloud into a microphone (Kawashima & Matsuyama, 2005).

None of this denies that g may have some basis in brain physiology. No doubt, natural selection has favored genetic upgrading of the primate brain over time and some people will have better genes for overall brain potential than others. Perhaps, right from conception, they have synapses that react more strongly to dopamine and, therefore, learn faster from repeated use. Blair (2006) emphasizes that cognition is linked to brain structures that underlie emotional reactions and stress. He presents ample evidence that physical trauma to these structures and early childhood emotional trauma, such as chronic neglect, can undermine an individual's problem-solving skills.

There are less dramatic environmental factors that cause individual differences in brain quality, such as nutrition and aerobic exercise. Cohen (2005) cites evidence that rhythmic use of large muscle groups stimulates the production of chemicals that, in turn, cause primitive brain cells to develop into neurons. It increases the number of connections in the frontal part of the brain, perhaps by increasing the networks of fine blood vessels in those regions. Good nutrition helps the entire body but there is some evidence that fish, olive oil, citrus fruits, and vegetables, combined with avoidance of saturated fat, is particularly beneficial to the brain (Melton, 2005). This too may be the result of improved blood supply to the brain.

Blair and Maguire show that functional autonomy in the brain seems to match the functional autonomy various mental skills exhibited in IQ gains over time. On both levels, on-the-spot problem-solving skills are relatively independent of the kind of crystallized skills exhibited in vocabulary, general information, and arithmetic. Therefore, no paradox appears to be looming when we move from the social to the brain levels. Imagine our concern if brain physiology showed that what happens on the social level, namely, various cognitive skills swimming freely of g, was impossible. But is the absence of a paradox a good thing? After all, paradoxes spurred progress towards integrating the social and the individual differences levels.

How much has g contributed to our knowledge of the brain?

A good theoretical construct should not only be fecund on its own level but also generate interesting hypotheses on other levels. We have seen that g has a good record on the social level but what about the brain level? The main research program that g-ocentric theory has pioneered on the brain level has to do with finding correlations between g and elementary cognitive tasks (ECTs). These tasks all measure the speed of your reactions after you have been presented with a "signal" to react. For example, they will time how long it takes each person to lift her finger off a button after she sees a flash of light (see Box 7). Then they will rank all of their subjects in terms of quickness of Reaction Time and compare that to their ranking on a highly g-loaded test like Raven's. They get a positive correlation which means the people who are quickest on the task tend to be above average for IQ although, depending on the task, the correlations are fairly modest ranging from .2 to .4.

This research poses two interlocked hypotheses: that we will see a meaningful pattern in the correlations between performance on heavily g-loaded tests (like Raven's) and performance on elementary cognitive tasks (ECTs); and that since performances on ECTs are indicators of the quality of brain processes, this will lead to physiological insights. For a moment, we will put the second hypothesis aside and explore the first.

The construct that is supposed to tie together the ECTs and g is that brighter people have a faster "mental speed." We have acknowledged that there may be a general factor, which arises

---

Box 7

The main elementary cognitive tasks are Reaction Time and Inspection Time.

A good example of Reaction Time is odd-button-out. You have your finger on a home button; above that, there are three target buttons with lights adjacent; either two target buttons light up and you go as quickly as you can to press the third; or one target button lights up and you go to press it. The total time it takes can be divided into Decision Time (how long it took to release the home button) and Movement Time (the time it took to go from the home button to the target button).

Inspection Time presents you with a simple pattern that is not symmetrical in that either the right side is not a solid line (I!) or the left side is not solid (!I). Just after one of these is flashed on a screen, a pattern appears that covers it up. The object is to establish the minimum time you need to distinguish I! from !I.

As for average evoked potentials (AEPs), the brains of people with different IQs have differently shaped "brain waves" when the brain gives an electrical response to a sudden change in sound. Electrodes are glued to the surface of the scalp and when the atypical sound is heard, the pattern of the brain's response is recorded by way of a graph of a certain shape.

---

from genetic superiority and better nutrition and more physical exercise, that gives some people brains with more potential than others. Faster "brain" reactions to stimuli may be a symptom of whose neural connections are more efficient. And that in turn may be a sign of whose neural connections will be more strengthened by cognitive exercise, which when translated into psychological language equates with those who learn better and faster (who are more intelligent).

In other words, people who do better on ECTs may have an advantage of this kind: when certain neurons spray dopamine in the area surrounding them, the synapses in the vicinity that have recently been active will be more sensitive to the dopamine. Therefore, they will be strengthened to a greater degree. When we get the capacity for fine-grained observation of the brain, we should check it out. Given what we know of brain physiology, would we not be inclined to do that anyway? Perhaps this is churlish and ECT research demands acknowledgment of a historical debt. But if nothing more seems to be forthcoming except reiterations of this insight, perhaps we should move on.

As to whether anything more specific has emerged from ECT research, Deary (2001, pp. 64–65) remarks that it has produced no consensus as to how to measure mental speed. Some prefer Reaction Times (how quickly you can release a home button and proceed to a target button), some prefer Inspection Time (how quickly you become aware of a visual perception), and some prefer AEPs (the brain's electrical response to stimuli) – look back to Box 7. Deary notes that it would be an odd theory that could be tested without a common yardstick and that, at present, results from the three yardsticks do not tally very well. There may seem to be a simple way of choosing: pick the one that gives the highest correlations with g. That, of course, would be an admission of theoretical bankruptcy.

Deary and Crawford (1998) analyze three data sets that disturbed them deeply. They all show negative correlations, ranging from –.315 to –.849, between the g loadings of WAIS-R (Wechsler Adult Intelligence Scale – Revised) subtests and Inspection Time and Word Identification respectively, two measures of "mental speed." These results, so troubling for g-ocentric theory, find a ready explanation if we approach brain physiology without the preconception of high centralization of cognitive processes.

The picture of the brain that has emerged is that of specific neural clusters developed in accord with the social priorities of the day, with some people advantaged by general factors such as better blood supply and greater dividends from cognitive exercise. This combination would tend to generate a g pattern on the individual differences level when people take the various Wechsler subtests. And it would tend to generate a positive correlation between ECTs and subtest g loadings if ECTs were all measures of the general factors that advantage some individuals over others.

Deary's results indicate that this is not the case. It looks as if various ECTs are linked to various neural clusters, perhaps Reaction Time to cluster A, Inspection Time to cluster B, and so forth. This would also explain Deary's observation that Reaction Time, Inspection Time, and AEPs do not all seem to be measures of a common metric one could call "mental speed." Another possibility that will be explored shortly is that ECTs are only weakly linked to physiological process and are more strongly linked to psychological processes like caution, self-confidence, and distractibility.

Nettelbeck (1998) has serious reservations about ECT research. Performance on both Reaction Time and Inspection Time improves only up through ages 11 to 14, while mental ability goes on developing long after adolescence. ECT performance is enhanced by practice. Green and Bavelier (2003) found that students who had played video games (Grand Theft Auto 3, Spiderman, and 007) were extraordinarily quick at counting the number of objects flashed on a screen and at correctly identifying two objects flashed in quick succession. These tasks bear a close resemblance to Inspection Time. Some individuals in the retardate IQ range have quick Inspection Times. Where poor performance does occur, it may be primarily a result of the fact that low-IQ subjects have a short attention span.

Some individuals who have quick Inspection Times have very low IQs indeed. Springer (2006) has described the work Matsuzawa has done with a chimpanzee named Ali. Ali has learned the numbers from zero to 9 in the sense that he knows that 3 refers to either three oranges or three boxes and so forth. He cannot create numbers, that is, he cannot grasp the concept that if you keep on adding one to the previous number, you can get as many numbers as you want. But if 7, 1, 3, 9, and 5 all pop up on a screen together helter-skelter, he will type them out in the proper order.

Matsuzawa then discovered something extraordinary. When the numbers are masked (covered over) at lightning speed, Ali can still register four or five and order them correctly. Human subjects (often scientists) are barely able to handle one or two. This chimpanzee is not only faster at Inspection Time than humans but also extremely consistent. The contest is not quite fair, of course. Ali gets a handful of raisins as a reward. The scientists can only hope to prove themselves more intelligent than a chimpanzee.

Between-species differences are not the same as within-species differences. For all we know, leopards are faster at ECTs than both apes and humans. Matsuzawa speculates that our brains have become specialized in a way that forfeits some Inspection Time speed to allow for more investment in higher cognitive functions. Nonetheless Ali engenders skepticism as to whether there is the functional relationship between excellence at ECTs and intelligence necessary to further knowledge of brain physiology.

Thus far, I have not directly confronted the second hypothesis that underpins this kind of research: that performance on ECTs gives us a measure, albeit an indirect measure, of neural efficiency. I think that this hypothesis stands on the brink of falsification. If it is falsified, ECT research is merely finding correlations between g and psychological phenomena of little importance and no real insight on the physiological level can be expected. As for AEPs (the electrical response of the brain), I have nothing to add to Callaway (1975) who argued that these can be influenced by personal factors including motivation and mood. Therefore, I will focus on Reaction Time and Inspection Time.

Using data collected by Lynn, Chan, and Eysenck (1991), Flynn (1991b) showed that cultural attitudes and strategy affect Reaction Time performance. This emerged most clearly in the odd-button-out Reaction Time task. As we saw in Box 7, the subjects have their finger on a home button and are confronted by three target buttons with lights corresponding to each. When only one light goes on or when only one remains unlit, they must release the home button and go to press the correct target button as quickly as they can. In other words, you can get two measurements: Decision Time (the time it takes to release the home button) and Movement Time (once the home button is released, the time it takes to reach the target button).

Chinese children turned out to be risk takers. As soon as there is a flash of light, Chinese children take their finger off the home button and "think" their way to the correct target button. On the other hand, British children are cautious. They will not leave the home button until they "know" which target button they are to arrive at. The result, of course, is that Chinese children are faster on Decision Time and British children are faster on Movement Time. For Chinese children, the correlation between Raven's IQ and Movement Time is the higher because it is when they are moving that they do their thinking. For British children, it is the reverse. The correlation between Raven's IQ and Decision Time is the higher because they are doing their thinking before they release the home button.

In other words, each nationality is faster at the task that most correlates with IQ for the other. If we were to take the connection between Reaction Time performance and physiological processes seriously, we would have to conclude that the British have better Chinese brains than the Chinese, while Chinese have better British brains than the British. These results suggest a research design.

Design I The hypothesis is that groups that do poorly on Reaction Times at present would do better if given the proper incentives. Therefore, the odd-button-out Reaction Time task will be modified into the "Point guard basketball game." Two subjects will face one another, each with a home button separated from three target buttons corresponding to three lights. The lights are synchronized and when the odd-button-out situation occurs, the subject who gets to the correct target button first has found "an open forward" who scores a basket worth two points. The winner is the one who has the most points after a sequence of 100 trials. In Britain, the game could be the "Find the open striker game," with a goal being registered after five successes over your opponent in a row.

Various mixes of competitors would be interesting: black versus white, male versus female, black male versus white female, lower IQ versus higher IQ. I would predict that the greatest competitive advantage would occur when black males face white females. Also that if low-IQ subjects face high-IQ subjects of the same gender and race, the greater variance in Reaction Time performance for the former would tend to diminish. If these hypotheses are supported, it will be established that many psychological factors influence Reaction Time performance: not just a propensity toward risk taking, but also confidence (blacks are pretty confident about their superiority over whites at basketball) and self-discipline in remaining attentive (something low-IQ subjects may normally lack).

It is fortuitous that Reaction Time involves two measurable tasks, Decision Time and Movement Time. But there is no reason why we could not investigate a unitary task like Inspection Time. An appropriate research design would be the following.

Design II The hypothesis is that a cautious subject will be at a disadvantage even on a unitary ECT such as Inspection Time. First, test a large sample of subjects on odd-button-out Reaction Time. From these, select two subsamples. Group A and Group B have the same overall time on the task, but Group A was slower to release the home button and Group B was quicker. Then test both groups on Inspection Time. Group A ought to do worse on Inspection Time simply because they are more cautious.

If the results of these two research designs show that ECTs are well removed from brain physiology, that plus the theoretical sterility of the ECT results so far would raise questions about how much time should be spent on ECT research. In any event, g does not seem to have any new hypotheses to put on the brain level. To be fair, I cannot think of anything to add to the hypotheses already put from the social level: the importance of current cognitive environment (cognitive exercise) and the functional independence of many cognitive abilities. I suspect that fecund methodologies like those of Blair and Cohen will have to supply us with more knowledge of the brain on the physiological level before we can make much progress.

Does g have competition?

I want to stress that the BIDS approach does not aim at the abolition of g. It merely endorses a separation of powers that gives each dominant construct the potency needed to rebuff the other two. The US Constitution attempts to make the President, Congress, and Supreme Court each dominant in the executive, legislative, and judicial areas. I want the same kind of federalism for the three levels of intelligence.

Like all organizing concepts, g must meet challenges posed on its own level, that is, the level of individual differences. There is no doubt that g is a good predictor of academic performance and quickness to profit from on-the-job training in many work roles. It sets effective IQ thresholds for various jobs and few who score below them will get those jobs. These thresholds rise as the cognitive complexity of work increases, ranging from skilled worker up to the elite professions. It is correlated with

SES (socio-economic status) and much social pathology. It is even a good predictor in surprising situations: recall that making a soufflé is more g loaded than scrambling eggs.

Daniel Goleman (1995) says that g or IQ must be supplemented by EQ (an Emotional Intelligence Quotient). He defines EQ as self-control, zeal, persistence, self-motivation, and sustaining hope. There is also a strong emphasis on self-knowledge and empathy (Goleman, 1998). This crosses the border between intelligence and wisdom. Some virtues of Aristotle's person of practical wisdom are there but others are missing, such as humane ideals and critical acumen. Perhaps this is because Goleman is addressing those who care less about the good life than academic and career success. Too much critical awareness and idealism are sometimes counterproductive in attaining those goals.

Heavily g-loaded IQ tests predict about 25 percent of the variance in academic success and on-the-job performance. Character is one of the missing pieces and there is a long history of trying to measure personality traits beginning with Thorndike (1920), who introduced the concept of social intelligence. There is no doubt that such traits are important. Duckworth and Seligman (2005) gave 164 American children an IQ test at the beginning of the eighth grade (age 13). The children also filled out a questionnaire about self-control and questionnaires solicited the opinions of their parents and teachers. To test their ability to delay gratification, they were given a dollar bill in an envelope: they could either open it or give it back unopened a week later and get two dollars. The results show that children's capacity for self-control has twice the weight of their IQs in predicting their grades.

Kelley and Caplan (1993) found that the members of Bell Laboratory research teams all had high IQs. But what distinguished star from average performers was not still higher IQ but effective interpersonal strategies. Heckman and Rubenstein (2001) compared dropouts who qualify for a high-school diploma by way of a general educational development exam (GEDs) and high-school dropouts who receive no diploma whatsoever. Although the GEDs had higher cognitive skills than the other dropouts, they earned no higher wages because they had lower non-cognitive skills. The market so penalized them for the latter that their cognitive advantage could not claw back the deficit. Heckman, Stixrud, and Urzua (2006) have since shown that non-cognitive factors, like self-esteem and the degree of control people feel they have over their fate, are just as important, if not more important, than cognitive skills for a whole range of outcomes. They affect not only wages and productivity on the job but also teenage pregnancy, smoking, marijuana use, and criminal behavior.

Do the current EQ tests, including Goleman's "emotional competence inventory," do any better than Duckworth and Seligman's informal techniques of measurement, or Heckman's use of the RLCS (Rotter Locus of Control Scale) and the RS-ES (Rosenberg's Self-Esteem Scale)? My own reading of the literature leaves me in doubt. Sternberg (1999) believes Goleman has done a good job of popular education but has similar reservations about his test. I see no reason in principle why these tests should not improve with time. However, it would be unfair to count their success as devaluing g.

The champions of g have never claimed that it measures important non-cognitive traits. They might be accused of over-estimating the extent to which those traits are correlated with g. If so, Jensen (1998, p. 573) is no longer subject to the indictment. He recognizes that largely uncorrelated with g, there exists a "general character factor" that arises out of analysis of a bundle of traits including constancy, perseverance, trustworthiness, conscientiousness, and kindness on principle. As a moral philosopher, I much prefer Jensen's list to that of Goleman. It is much closer to what one needs to live a good life.

Sternberg (1988) offers a much more serious challenge. He acknowledges that g has a good record but believes that it has exhausted its scientific potential even on the level of individual differences. This amounts to a claim that g-ocentric theory is no longer fecund in generating interesting new hypotheses and needs to be supplanted by other constructs. Sternberg calls g "the academic form of intelligence" and has formulated a triarchic theory of intelligence.

"Analytic intelligence" is close to what traditional tests measure as fluid g, that is, solving abstract problems on the spot as in Raven's. "Creative intelligence" tries to go beyond Raven's to test on-the-spot creativity of a less cerebral sort, for example, selecting cartoons with blank captions for the characters and filling in what would be appropriate and clever, or writing impromptu stories on themes like the octopus's sneakers. "Practical intelligence" is an attempt to measure skills used to apply concepts to real-world contexts. For example, how to deal with writing a recommendation for someone you do not know well, handling a competitive work situation, or how to deal with a difficult room mate. Its measurable core is tacit knowledge. The latter is very close to the capacity of Aristotle's person of practical wisdom to find the golden mean between two extremes. Some people, whether by nature or by habituation, are much better than others at determining what ought to be done on the battle-field, rather than being too cautious or too rash.

It is early days yet to see whether Sternberg's tests can be vindicated in terms of external validity. He cites a few studies that seem to show that his test betters g as a predictor of real-world performance in work situations (Sternberg et al., 2000). However, as Gottfredson (2001) points out, these must be replicated and much supplemented before he can make a solid claim. His most impressive achievement has to do with prediction of university grade point averages (GPAs). By adding his triarchic measures to the traditional predictive variables of high-school grades and SAT (Scholastic Aptitude Test) scores, he increased the percentage of variance explained from .159 to .248 (Sternberg, 2006). Which is to say that the correlation between the predictive measures and university grades increased from .40 to .50.

Jensen (1998) shows strong resistance to Sternberg's measures. It seems obvious to me that they measure skills that help predict things like how interesting a student's essays will strike university staff. I cannot see how the potency they add to predictive validity threatens g's proud record on the individual differences level.

Some advice for IQ test organizations

Whatever the merits of Goleman's and Sternberg's proposals, there is one area in which I believe it very important to supplement measures of "academic" intelligence with a different measure. As we have seen, present IQ tests downgrade using intelligence on the concrete level in favor of using intelligence on the formal operational level. It is arguable that someone competent on the concrete level can cope with everyday life. If so, an inability to cope on the formal level will have the lesser significance that they cannot cope with school subjects. If we could disentangle the two competencies, we might be better able to determine when to use the label "mentally retarded" and when to use "learning disability." At present, the line is often drawn in terms of what parents will resent least. Therefore, I will propose a third research design.

Design III Children who score as mentally retarded on the WISC should take a Piagetian test to determine whether or not they are competent on the level of concrete reality. If the language could be simplified and yet the focus on concrete problems retained, something like Bond's Logical Operations Test (the BLOT) might discriminate between WISC items that can be handled by someone competent on the concrete level and those items that cannot. If so, they would provide a key that would make individual administration of the Piagetian test unnecessary.

All subjects would try all the WISC items and get an IQ score. But we would also assign a CC score based purely on the items a subject can attack based on concrete competence. The CC score would have to pass all of the tests of external validity. The most fundamental of these would be whether those who get above 70 for CC but below 70 for IQ seem competent to deal with everyday life, that is, whether they can follow the rules of baseball even though they are having academic difficulties.

Finally, a reservation about how IQ tests are evolving. The Wechsler and Stanford–Binet organizations are designing their tests more and more to measure the latent traits of factor analysis. Since they want to measure individual differences, and that is the kingdom of factor analysis, I cannot object. But on the social level, the dominant concept is social utility and what we want are measures of real-world functional skills that have great social significance. The ten core subtests the WISC-IV uses to measure Full Scale IQ no longer include Information and Arithmetic. Fortunately, both tests were still normed on the WISC-IV standardization sample and a group who took them both was scored against both the WISC-III and WISC-IV norms. This gave us an estimate of trends on Information and Arithmetic between 1989 and 2002. The psychological corporations should seek a grant to continue this practice. Otherwise, a priceless record of trends, extending all of the way from 1947–1948 to the present, is in danger of extinction.

Prolegomena to the advancement of knowledge

I am too much in love with philosophy to collect data or do field studies. Those still active who have done so much to advance our knowledge of intelligence will have to continue to do so (see Box 8).

The best I can hope to do is offer a framework that may help the physiologists, psychologists, and sociologists who walk down the evidential path. Perhaps they will not have to contend

---

Box 8

I put my faith in scholars like Clancy Blair, Steve Ceci, Roberto Colom, Ian Deary, Bill Dickens, Christopher Hallpike, Arthur Jensen, Nick Mackintosh, Charles Murray, Ted Nettelbeck, John Raven, Michael Shayer, Robert Sternberg, and Wendy Williams. I want to say that Georg Oesterdiekhoff brought a Piagetian interpretation of the past to my attention and was kind enough to correspond in English rather than in his native German. Fortunately, he is writing some books that will make his contribution accessible in English.

---

with roadblocks such as concern over defining intelligence and *g*'s tendency towards conceptual imperialism. It would be good if someone pursued the research designs recommended. I think we need to go beyond *g* despite its outstanding record of fecundity. I strongly recommend that we do not spend another decade publishing correlations between *g* and elementary cognitive tasks. But even in this, I may be mistaken:

> If someone is 60 percent right, it's wonderful, it's great luck and let him thank God. But ... whoever says he is 100 percent right is a fanatic, a thug, and the worse kind of rascal. (An old Jew of Galicia)

4 Testing the Dickens/Flynn model

> It is the mark of an educated man ... that in every subject he
> looks for only so much precision as its nature permits.
> (Aristotle, *Ethics*, i, 3, 1094b, 24–26)

Dickens and Flynn think that the Dickens/Flynn model is important. In Chapter 2, it was used to solve the paradox of how environment could appear so feeble in the twin studies and yet so potent
in IQ gains over time. Therefore, it stands as a serious attempt to
integrate the level of individual differences (twin studies) and
the level of social trends (IQ gains over time). At present, there
is no model that can claim to integrate the level of individual
differences and the level of brain physiology. If we get one, there
would be only one step left: the integration of those two models
into what would truly be a BIDS theory of intelligence. The model
is also important because it has implications for how IQ can be
enhanced.

Interventions and raising IQ

Interventions that may enhance IQ include the efforts of
parents, affording an enriched environment to children at risk,
adoption, and university study. It is important that parents do
their best by their children but they must reconcile themselves
to the fact that their efforts cannot be decisive in the long term.

The Dickens/Flynn model posits a tug of war between two
environments: the environment parents impose, which is not

directly correlated with the child's unique genetic endowment; and the environment the child creates by interacting with the world, which does tend to match the child's unique genetic endowment. With each passing year, a child transcends parental influence and becomes an autonomous actor. Moreover, a child's genetic endowment for IQ is always with him or with her, while quality of environment is much more at the mercy of life history. Parents cannot prevent their child from rebelling against a teacher with whom there is little rapport or getting in with the wrong crowd. Therefore, there is a strong tendency for a genetic advantage or disadvantage to get more and more matched to a corresponding environment. The child who finds schoolwork easy is more likely to see it as a way to excel, become motivated to do more homework, and get extension work from teachers. The child who has to strain to keep up is more likely to get discouraged and spend more time on sport than studies.

In either event, over the school years, the imposed parental environment uncorrelated with genes loses ground to the acquired environment correlated with genes. The fact that family environment loses ground with age is confirmed by the twin studies. The genetic proportion of IQ variance rises with age from 45 percent in childhood to 75 percent in adulthood. The "common environment" portion of IQ variance falls from 30 percent to practically zero. The latter mainly reflects living in this family rather than that family.

Preschool interventions also impose an environment on children that is uncorrelated with their genes, usually a uniformly enriched one that includes stimulation through educational toys, books, contact with sub-professionals, and so forth. If these terminate as children enter school, the intervention is likely to lose the tug of war even earlier than a child's parents do. After all, the parents retain some influence after the preschool years. A child emerging from a preschool intervention is thrown on his or her own resources at school and there will be a gradual tendency for the child's genetic endowment to re-emerge and start the matching process. Since the imposed environment was far more enriched than any available at school, the child will begin to match environments that get further and further below its quality. Therefore the intervention's IQ bonus will tend to decline. What would happen if a significant intervention were sustained to adulthood is unknown.

The most radical form of environmental intervention is adoption into a privileged home. Adoptive parents often wonder why the adopted child loses ground to their natural children. If their own children inherit elite genes and the adopted child has average genes, then as parents slowly loose the ability to impose an equally enriched environment on both, the individual differences in genes begin to dominate. Finally, note that university education is a partial attempt to impose an enriched environment on students regardless of their genetic differences, that is, it constitutes a quasi-environmental intervention on the adult level. It too will see its effects on IQ fade unless quality of environment is maintained, for example, unless, thanks to a good university education, a student of average ability qualifies for a cognitively demanding profession. Then the job takes over the university's role of imposing duties that foster the intellect. The non-IQ effects of university education are much more likely to be permanent than the IQ effects. The contacts made at a good university may confer an enhanced income and SES throughout life.

None of the above applies mechanically to group differences. The mere fact that different ethnic groups attended the same schools and yet emerge with different IQs does not mean that the IQ difference between the groups is genetic in origin. The different subcultures of groups affect both of the two environments competing with one another in the tug of war. Parents in both groups may impose an early environment that ignores genetic differences between their children, but if the parents in one group are largely poor solo-parents, children from the two groups may enter school with very different IQs. If other environmental handicaps take over at each stage of life history – a teenage subculture that is atypical linguistically and more prone to gang membership, an adult world in which many go to prison and most have jobs that make few cognitive demands – then an environmentally induced IQ gap between the two groups will persist into old age.

How we can enhance our mental abilities

These comments about interventions may seem to imply that no one can really hope to improve on his or her genetic endowment. This pessimism is no more in order than pessimism about whether people can improve on their physical endowment for running. To do so, you must either have good luck or make your own luck. Either a happy chain of circumstances will force you to train throughout your life or you can develop a love for running and train without compulsion. Training will not override genes entirely, of course. There are runners I cannot beat even when I train more than they do. But I can run rings around every couch potato within twenty years of my age.

As we have seen, the cognitive advantages of a good childhood environment tend to be lost once the child becomes autonomous. You can always hope that your children will have good luck in the sense that "surrogate parents" provide them with what amounts to a favorable environmental intervention throughout life. But tracing a life history of that sort will show how chancy that is.

A girl is born with average genes for cognitive ability in a privileged home. Her parents give her books, help with homework, and make sure she has a positive attitude to school. As she becomes a teenager, she goes to a good high school and is fortunate enough to make friends most of whom aspire to professional careers, so school plus peers take over the parents' role of imposing a stimulating environment. She gets the marks needed for entry into a decent university. She has to work harder than most but she has her heart set on getting into law school. Her marks get her in without much to spare but, once there, she profits from the fact that no one with a reasonable education who works hard fails to graduate. She is lucky enough to get into a good firm where she has challenging work and she marries a colleague with intellectual interests.

If her friends from college, her workmates, her husband, and her husband's friends dominate her social interaction, they might constitute a sort of "cocoon" that gave her a sheltered cognitive environment just as her parents did when she was a small child. This would be very rare. She would need very good luck indeed to enjoy an externally imposed stimulating environment that lasted throughout her life. Note that even if she marries a fool and regresses toward his level intellectually, he and she may be wealthy fools, so her good start has given her permanent affluence if not permanent mental acuity.

However, there is one way in which individuals can make their own luck. He or she can internalize the goal of seeking challenging cognitive environments – seeking intellectual challenges all the way from choosing the right leisure activities to wanting to marry someone who is intellectually stimulating. The best chance of enjoying enhanced cognitive skills is to fall in love with ideas, or intelligent conversation, or intelligent books, or some intellectual pursuit. If I do that, I create within my own mind a stimulating mental environment that accompanies me wherever I go. Then I am relatively free of needing good luck to enjoy a rich cognitive environment. I have constant and instant access to a portable gymnasium that exercises the mind. Books and ideas and analyzing things are easier to transport than a basketball court. No one can keep me from using mental arithmetic so habitually that my arithmetical skills survive.

This advice is not based on mere wishful thinking. Ross (2006) summarizes a wide range of studies as to how chess grandmasters can perform their remarkable feats such as playing forty games at once while blindfolded. What differentiated them from other expert players did not seem to be raw talent but persistence in seeking cognitive challenges. After making the effort to master chess to a certain level, most of us relax. Others never desist from "effortful study," that is, from continuously taking on challenges that lie just beyond their competence.

The only secure path to maximizing one's intelligence is to capture a rich cognitive environment and hide it within, where it will be safe. Perhaps this is as it should be: those who value intelligence for its own sake have the best chance to view the world through intelligent eyes. I must add that this kind of self-improvement is compatible with the Dickens/Flynn model as distinct from being explicit within it.

Testable facets of the model

If the model is important, it is important to test it. To determine what evidence is relevant, I will review some of the important facets of the model.

IA. **The individual multiplier**. By using the individual multiplier, the model shows how, at a given time, a small genetic advantage on the part of an individual captures powerful environmental forces. Recall how feedback loops take a small genetic advantage and, by matching it to increasingly enhanced environments, multiply its effects.

IB. **Genes versus environment**. Therefore, the Dickens/Flynn model alters the balance between the potency of genes and environment in favor of environment. In principle, this difference between it and conventional models should be testable.

IIA. **Environmental decay**. As indicated, environmental quality must be maintained throughout life history, which is to say that current environment swamps previous environments and that the latter quickly become weaker as they recede into the past. There are exceptions, of course: being crushed by a 20-ton truck will have permanent effects.

IIB. **Transitory vs. persistent**. Therefore, any research design that can assess whether the effects of environment are transitory or persistent will test the Dickens/Flynn model.

IIIA. **The social multiplier**. By using the social multiplier, the model shows how environment can have an immense cumulative impact on IQ over time. Recall how feedback loops take an environmental event that boosts the average IQ and make the rising average IQ a potent force in its own right. Individuals throughout the whole society, unless something renders them socially isolated, react to the rising mean in a way that boosts their own IQs, which raises the mean IQ higher, and away you go.

IIIB. **Spillover effects**. Therefore, any research design that can assess whether high IQ in one sector of society spills over to boost IQ among others, rather than remaining compartmentalized, will test the Dickens/Flynn model.

Genes versus environment

Flynn thought he had a straightforward test of this facet of the model. Let us go back to the estimates of the heritability of IQ based on kinship data. Conventional models take at face value 75 percent as the heritability of IQ for adults and, therefore, leave only 25 percent of IQ variance for environment. Our model says that the 75 percent is divided between the direct effect of genes on IQ (let us say on the quality of brain inherited) and the indirect effect on IQ genes acquire through co-opting powerful environmental factors by way of matching. Note that the heritability of IQ in young children is only 45 percent and even they have already done some matching of their peculiar genetic quality to corresponding environments. Let us say that one-fifth of the value is due to matching. Then the direct effect of genes on IQ accounts for only 36 percent of IQ variance. This leaves 64 percent as the share for the indirect effect of genes plus environmental differences uncorrelated with genes.

Flynn wanted to take advantage of this difference between the models by controlling for IQ and deriving contrasting predictions. Actually, IQ would be controlled statistically, so what follows is simplified to convey the logic of the enterprise.

Assume we had a pair of identical twins, whose IQs differed by 5 points, and compared them to a pair of randomly selected individuals, whose IQs also differed by 5 points. Both pairs should be adults of the same age. Since the conventional model gives the genetic identity of the twins far more potency than the Dickens/Flynn model, it predicts that the within-pair environmental gap for the twins would be much larger than within-pair environmental difference for the randomly selected individuals. We would predict a smaller ratio between the two gaps. The two predictions can be quantified: they would predict that the within-pair environmental gap for the identical twins would have to be twice as great; we would predict that it would only have to be only 1.4 times as great (see Box 9).

Assume we had an environmental index that included all factors likely to affect IQ and we had the environmental data about the members of a sample needed to put it to work. We would then select unrelated individuals at random and put them into pairs in the order selected. With our index and our data, we could then estimate the within-pair environmental gap of unrelated

Box 9

Derivation of the two predictions:

(1) Convention puts the percentage of adult IQ variance attributable to environment at .25. The square root of that is .50, which stands as the correlation between IQ and environment.

(2) This entails a ratio of 2 : 1 between environment and IQ, that is, if the environmental gap between two individuals increases by one SD, their IQs will diverge by 0.5 SDs.

(3) In our model, environment has a greater impact. The ratio is 1.4 : 1, that is, an environmental increase of one SD will increase the IQ gap by 0.714 SDs (1.00 divided by .714 = 1.4).

(4) Take a pair of individuals randomly selected from a normal distribution. They will be uncorrelated for everything: genes, environment, and IQ. Their typical IQ gap will be 16.926 points and their environmental gap will be the same (measured in terms of the common metric of SDs).

(5) Assume (just to make the point) that we find a pair of identical twins separated by 16.932 points. Also assume that we can measure environmental gaps.

(6) Then, the conventional model predicts that the within-pair environmental gap for the twins will be twice that for the randomly selected individuals; and the Dickens/Flynn model predicts that the ratio would be only 1.4 : 1.

individuals, estimate the within-pair environmental gap of identical twins, and compare the two gaps. If the within-pair IQ difference was the same for the twins and the randomly selected individuals, we could test our prediction (that the within-pair environmental gap for twins would be 1.4 times as great) against the conventional prediction (that it would be twice as great).

As for sample sizes, a reasonable allowance for measurement error dictates a sample size of 100 for each kind of pair. However, there is an escape hatch from the results of this research design. If twin pairs do not exhibit the large environmental gap that conventional models posit, it might be the fault of the index of environmental quality. Assume that the index is missing potent environmental influences on IQ and contains mainly factors of lesser importance. It would then give unreliable measurements of the ratio between the sizes of various environmental gaps.

But we could still draw a conclusion of great significance: either the Dickens/Flynn model is correct; or we are unable to identify the specific environmental factors that affect IQ. There is an irony here. Usually, it is those who argue for a large environmental influence on IQ who must resort to a plea of ignorance about the nature of specific factors. And those inclined to genetic determinism take pleasure in their discomfort. It would be nice to have the shoe on the other foot. It would be the genetic school that would have to plead environmental ignorance to avoid embarrassment. This might eliminate point scoring and unite us in a search for better knowledge.

Then came disappointment. As so often occurs, Dickens concluded that Flynn's notion was unworkable (we do not immediately agree on everything). He developed our model to distinguish between the effect of genes on environment through affecting IQ and though other paths. And he allowed for measurement error in calculating environmental differences. His conclusion: it was no longer possible to derive unique predictions from the two models. The nice tidy predictions of $2:1$ vs. $1.4:1$ had disappeared in a welter of complications. I have to accept such things as demonstrated but am reluctant to give up. The difference between our model and the conventional model in terms of the potency of environment seems such an obvious point of comparison. We would both welcome anyone who sees a way forward that we have missed.

Transitory versus persistent

Dickens notes that the prediction our model makes about the transitory effects of environmental change is virtually unique. Take someone who makes a new friend who is intellectually stimulating or takes up a hobby that is more cognitively demanding (chess). At that point, that person's cognitive abilities should start to rise and multiply. But most people do not sustain a friendship or hobby throughout life. Rather these things come and go and when they go, there should be a negative impact on IQ so that it begins to decay. In other words, our model posits that cognitive ability should fluctuate in tandem with positive or negative influences on someone's IQ. The consequence of rejecting our model, or any similar model, is the presumption that the effects of environmental change would be either permanent or completely transient.

It would be rewarding to compare identical twins that have experienced different environmental shocks, for example, one is drafted for three years while the other remains at university. The different environmental events should create a sharp widening of the IQ gap between them that gradually fades way after they both return to normal life. We could measure just how long it took their IQ gap to converge to the pre-shock level.

Another use for identical twins. Since they have identical genes, whenever you measure the gap between their IQs, you are measuring something purely environmental in origin. The environmental difference between the twins will vary from year to year if only because two individuals never have identical life histories. Our model posits that the effects of these differential environmental events will be transitory, so the correlations between the IQ gaps that separate a pair of twins will show a long-term tendency to lessen over time. That is, if you compare the IQ gaps over an interval of merely one year, you will get a higher correlation than when you compare the gap of 2000 with that of 2005. There will be some continuity, particularly in adulthood, where continuity of environment is anchored by occupational continuity. Nonetheless, we would predict an exponential decline in the magnitude of the correlation over time.

Those who think that current environment has lasting effects would anticipate a high degree of correlation for identical twin IQ gaps even when those gaps were separated by many years. The more that environmental factors have some permanent effect, the more the differential environmental events of a given year should have effects on IQ that linger on after many years.

Spillover effects of academics

The social multiplier posits that other people are the most important feature of our cognitive environment and that the mean IQ of our social environment is a potent influence on our own IQ. Therefore, unless you are part of a very isolated group, whether you live in a high- or low-IQ community should affect your IQ. Moreover, if there is a cognitively elite group in your city or town, their high IQ should have effects that spill over to the whole community. These spillover effects are the footprints that a social multiplier leaves in the sand of IQ data.

Being an academic, Flynn proposed a research design than looks for the spillover effects a university should have on its home town or city (assuming, of course, that the university is staffed by something that deserves to be called a cognitive elite). Any state would do, but the design focuses on Wisconsin.

Design IV (1) The cities and towns of Wisconsin could be ranked by the percentage of their population that attends or is employed by universities. I suspect the ranking would go from Madison (a small city dominated by the University of Wisconsin) to Milwaukee (a larger city where the university is also present plus many other professionals) to Whitewater (which has a state college – I leave it open as to whether state college populations should get the full weight of a university population) to Janesville (which has no tertiary institution – as I recall). (2) We would compare the IQ scores of every child who moved from one city to another in terms of their before and after IQs. Since the comparisons are child by child, we are controlling for genes. (3) The prediction would be that transferring from low to high on the city hierarchy would be positive, from high to low negative, and the greater the distance on the hierarchy the greater the effect.

This design has the advantage that data are readily available, assuming there are IQ or "aptitude" test data uniform from city to city, and that schools inherit data when a child transfers and have on record the child's last school. Schools would not, of course, release data that identified a particular child's IQ, but the data could be coded to preserve anonymity.

As an alternative, you could rank school districts by mean IQ or by the district's average on the Scholastic Aptitude Test (SAT). Children who transfer from a high- to a low-IQ school district should show an IQ loss. This would seem to demonstrate a spillover effect linking the schools in a particular school district. However, there would probably be many confounding variables, such as high-IQ school districts having more qualified teachers and so forth. If you found cities whose only difference was the presence of a tertiary institution, these confounding variables would be absent or at least they might be less prominent and more easily statistically controlled.

The presence of spillover effects between a university and the surrounding community would be a much more dramatic demonstration of the phenomenon. It also has the advantage of showing that the mere presence of university personnel is a salutary influence, something many might find it irritating to concede.

Spillover effects between age cohorts

Dickens notes that some models, unlike our own, do not posit a social multiplier. Take a model that attributes IQ gains basically to physiological causes (such as enhanced genes over time) and thus sidelines the social multiplier. Such a model would suggest a pattern of IQ gains that showed pure age cohort effects. If some children began to profit from better genes at a certain time, the children affected would begin to show IQ gains, but there would be no spillover to their parents or to other children who were older. The Dickens/Flynn model implies that this is false, that is, it predicts that IQ gains would not be compartmentalized in this way. The children with enhanced IQs would be part of the cognitive environment of their parents (they would challenge their parents with their greater intellectual curiosity), older siblings (their older siblings would be affected by playing computer games with them), teachers (they would keep their teachers on their toes), indeed, they would affect whoever came into contact with them.

Dickens (2004) has formulated a research design that would test models with a social multiplier against at least some models that lack one.

Design V The hypothesis is that, dating from their inception, IQ gains over time should not be age specific but should show spillover effects that produce gains at all ages. Precisely because they lack a social multiplier, most other models suggest that when IQ gains over time occur, different cohorts would show different levels of IQ without spillovers from one cohort to another. As for the evidence required, it would have to be longitudinal IQ data that followed cohorts over several decades, that is, the kind of data Schaie and Hertzog (1983) have been collecting.

Statistical techniques cannot distinguish between cohort trends, year gains, and trends due to the fact that people gain or lose ground on IQ as they age. However, if a social multiplier is present and its effects over time are changing, it is possible to detect its presence although not to estimate its magnitude. The pattern the data take under these conditions is complex and I can only refer the reader to Dickens (2004) and McKenzie (2006) for a description. But the footprint of a social multiplier, that is, spillover effects between cohorts, should be there. Dickens (2004) presents preliminary evidence that it is there for some measures of cognitive ability.

Factor loadings and age

Dickens notes that the emphasis of our model on people as the crucial facet of environment has an implication. Even though there are spillover effects between age cohorts, the way in which people reinforce one another's cognitive development does differ with age. Parental interaction with a young child differs from a retired person's interaction with their friends. Dickens (2004) has shown that the factor loadings (including the g loadings) of different Wechsler subtests could vary depending on the nature of an age group's social interaction.

For example, he believes that if we could order the cognitive demands of all the relevant environments along a single dimension, a big if, then we could note the skills that are most often used in the most demanding way. And these would be the skills with the highest g loadings. Therefore, there should be small but detectable shifts in the g loadings of various subtests with age, which is to say that there ought to be shifts between corresponding subtests as we go from the WISC (given to children) to the WAIS (given to adults).

Flynn investigated this by comparing the WISC-R (Rushton, 1995, p. 187) and WAIS subtests (Jensen, 1980, p. 218). There are some quite significant shifts between children and adults in the g-loading hierarchy. Block Design and Arithmetic fall from fourth and sixth highest down to a tie for eighth and ninth. Comprehension drops from fifth to seventh. Picture Completion, Object Assembly, and Picture Arrangement all rise from seventh, eighth, and ninth to fourth, fifth, and sixth. Only Vocabulary, Information, and Similarities hold their ground. It looks as if our social circles want us to be able to chat and discuss a reasonable range of topics at all ages; and as if the habit of classifying the world is shared by young and old.

It is also interesting that the average g loading of WAIS subtests is much higher than that of WISC subtests: .807 as compared to only .586. This may mean that the adult environment makes more uniform demands on the skills measured by the Wechsler tests, as compared to a childhood environment whose demands are relatively selective. If this is so, and if the environments of adults are more easily ordered along a single dimension of increasing cognitive demands, there would be a tendency for the ten subtests of the WAIS to be more highly correlated (and thus have higher g loadings) than the corresponding subtests of the WISC.

The data I have summarized are crude stuff. As usual, Dickens is far more cautious than Flynn and will not speculate on what skills might be more prominent at what age. However, I will speculate if only to exemplify the point. School-related cognitive skills would be more relevant for a 7-year-old and those used in bridge and poker more relevant for a 67-year-old retiree. As people age, the main group that constitutes their peers shifts from classmates to workmates to leisure companions. The last are always important but tend to dominate after retirement. Therefore, the demands put on our cognitive abilities must differ with age, from keeping up with the class, to seeking promotion at work, and finally to not being boring in old age.

Dickens emphasizes that the social interactions that reinforce different cognitive abilities do not merely fluctuate with age. People of the same age in different occupations have different cognitive environments, for example, take two lawyers one of whom stays at home for four years after having a child and the other of whom goes on working.

Testing everything

Evidencing all of the distinctive features of the Dickens/ Flynn model would require a longitudinal study of a large sample, with over-representation of twins, that accumulated data on their occupations, hobbies, and friends and tested their IQs yearly. It would be of maximum benefit if some subjects took part in experiments aimed at boosting their cognitive abilities, say, paying people to spend time playing a cognitively demanding computer game. Even better, some should play the game as part of a social group and others as isolated individuals.

As these comments indicate, testing the Dickens/Flynn model will take time. Those who are impatient should help. They can help by following our research designs, or propose better tests of our model, or best of all, develop alternative models that resolve the genes versus environment paradox. Lamenting that the model has not been tested since its inception does not count as help.

5   Why did it take so long?

> A basic lesson of sociology is that what happens within a social system is not completely determined by the individual characteristics of its members.
>
> (Carmi Schooler, "Environmental complexity and the Flynn effect," p. 72)

The reader may wonder why it took twenty years to solve our four paradoxes. The reason was that their solution lay in a comprehensive analysis of the social forces at work as society changes over time. I was distracted by three barriers to understanding all of which downplayed the role of social evolution. Two of them singled out highly specific social trends as central: a tendency toward social mobility and mating with a wider variety of partners; and a tendency toward better nutrition. The third was a methodological mistake that made social forces seem too feeble to explain much.

Tokyo and American history

What if enhanced genes over the last century was an important cause of IQ gains over time? If so, I have exaggerated the significance of cultural evolution. I do not think anyone would propose that genes have been enhanced by eugenic reproduction, that is, reproductive patterns caused by high-IQ people having more children than low-IQ people. In America, those with more education have had fewer offspring than those with less education throughout either most or all of the twentieth century. The current data suggest that reproductive patterns, perhaps reinforced by immigration, may have cost America about one IQ point per generation (Herrnstein & Murray, 1994, ch. 15; Lynn & Van Court, 2004). Lynn (1996b) argues that most other nations are similar.

That leaves hybrid vigor. A group's genes can benefit from outbreeding as an antidote to the deleterious effects of inbreeding. The latter is called inbreeding depression (IBD). The classic study of IBD and IQ is that of Schull and Neel (1965, Table 12.19). Jensen and Rushton cite their results as indicative of which WISC subtests are most sensitive to IBD. For example, the IQ deficit that inbred children suffer on the Vocabulary subtest is almost three times as great as the deficit they suffer on Coding (Jensen, 1983, Table 2; Rushton, 1995, Table 9.1).

Schull and Neel administered the WISC to 1,854 children in Hiroshima: 989 were outbred (their parents had no significant percentage of genes in common); and 865 were inbred, varying from being the issue of first-cousin marriages to second-cousin marriages. The measure of IBD is expressed in terms the size of the IQ deficit per 10 percent of inbreeding. Schull and Neel's data put IBD at 5 IQ points per 10 percent of inbreeding. American children gained about 18 IQ points between 1947 and 2002. For IBD to account for that gain, their percentage of inbreeding in 1947 would have to have been 36 percent (18 divided by $5 = 3.6$; that $\times 10\% = 36\%$). Children have half the genes in common that their parents share. Therefore, the typical parents of American children in 1947 had to have 72 percent of their genes in common.

Brothers and sisters share only 50 percent (actually a bit more due to assortive mating for IQ) of their genes. So it would not be enough if all children were the result of incest. Three-fifths of the children in 1947 would have to have been the fruit of incest and the other two-fifths the offspring of same-sex (by definition) identical twins.

Reverting to the real world, what would the percentage of inbreeding have to have been for hybrid vigor to explain even 4 or 5 percent of IQ gains from 1947 to 2002? American children in 1947 had to be inbred to the point that their parents were all analogous to second cousins (second cousins have 1.56 percent of their genes in common). That is hardly plausible. Moreover, there is strong evidence that hybrid vigor played no role at all. There is no significant correlation between which subtests are most affected by IBD and which show the largest IQ gains. Coding, Block Design, Object Assembly, Picture Arrangement, and Similarities show the largest IQ gains. In terms of IBD, they are scattered all over the hierarchy, that is, they come in at first (lowest), third, sixth, eighth and ninth places respectively (see Appendix I for Table 2 which presents Schull & Neel's data).

These results should come as no surprise. The notion that America was a collection of isolated communities that discovered geographical mobility only in the twentieth century is an odd reading of history. Americans never did live in small inbred groups. Right from the start, there was a huge influx of migrants who settled in both urban and rural areas. There were huge population shifts during settlement of the West, after the Civil War, and during the World Wars. The growth of mobility has been modest: in 1870, 23 percent of Americans were living in a state other than the one of their birth; in 1970, the figure was 32 percent (Mosler & Catley, 1998).

Norway and who was getting taller

Nutrition is an environmental factor but it is unusual. Most of the environmental factors I have deemed relevant to explaining IQ gains over time affect the brain much as exercise develops our muscles. However, if most people were once seriously undernourished, the capacity of their brains to respond to cognitive exercise might have been impaired and enhanced nutrition would emerge as the central causal factor of IQ gains.

Richard Lynn (1987, 1989) and Storfer (1990) have emph-
asized nutrition. I do not doubt that it plays an important role in
developing nations or that it did so even in America and Britain
before 1950. Between the late nineteenth century and the mid
twentieth century, there were significant advances in nutrition
and child health. Well-fed and healthy children learn better at
school and have more energy to learn during their leisure.
However, I am skeptical that health or nutrition contributed
much to IQ gains in America or the more prosperous European
nations in the era of post-1950 affluence.

Since 1950, the most dramatic health gains for children in
advanced nations have to do with care while the child is in the
womb, delivering infants at birth, and post-natal care including
that of premature babies. Rutter (2000, p. 223) argues persuasively
that these improvements have had no net effect. For every child
who has escaped mental impairment, an impaired child has been
saved who would have died without modern techniques.

As for nutrition, no one has actually shown that American
or British children have a better diet today than they did in 1950,
indeed, the critics of junk food argue that diets are worse. We have
noted the 20-point Dutch gain on a Raven's-type test registered
by military samples tested in 1952, 1962, 1972, and 1982. Did the
Dutch 18-year-olds of 1982 really have a better diet than the
18-year-olds of 1972? The former outscored the latter by fully 8 IQ
points. It is interesting that the Dutch 18-year-olds of 1962 did have
a known nutritional handicap. They were either in the womb or
born during the great Dutch famine of 1944 – when German troops
monopolized food and brought sections of the population to near
starvation. Yet, they do not show up even as a blip in the pattern of
Dutch IQ gains. It is as if the famine had never occurred (Flynn,
1987, p. 172).

In the absence of direct data, there are some indirect
criteria that allow us to test for the impact of better nutrition.
Presumably, the more affluent have had an adequate diet since

1950. Therefore, nutritional gains would benefit mainly the less affluent half of the population and IQ gains would be concentrated in the bottom half of the IQ curve. There are six nations for which we have the whole IQ distribution from top to bottom: France from 1949 to 1974; the Netherlands from 1952 to 1982; Denmark from 1958 to 1987; the US from 1948 to 1989; Spain from 1970 to 1999; and Norway from 1957 to 2002. Denmark, Spain, and Norway show larger gains in the bottom half of the curve, but the other three do not (Colom, Lluis Font, & Andres-Pueyo, 2005; Flynn, 1985, p. 240, 1987, Table 3; Teasdale & Owen, 1989, 2000; Sundet, Barlaug, & Torjussen, 2004; Vroon, 1984; Wechsler, 1992, Table 6.9).

Where we do not have the full distribution, a sign that gains might be concentrated in the lower half would be that the range of variance (the SD) of IQ scores has lessened over time. If the lower half has gained, and the upper half has not, clearly the bottom scores will come closer to the top scores. A survey of the better data sets shows that Belgium, Argentina, Sweden, Canada, New Zealand, and Estonia have no pattern of declining variance. In Israel, males show no decline but females do; however, the female data are inferior in quality and it is hardly plausible that the latter had a worse diet than the former (Bouvier, 1969, pp. 4–5; Clarke, Nyberg, & Worth, 1978, p. 130; Emanuelsson, Reuterberg, & Svensson, 1993; Flynn, 1987, Table 5, 1998b, Table 1a; Flynn & Rossi-Casé, under review; Must, Must, & Raudik, 2003).

Therefore, as far as we know, nutrition is viable as a causal factor in only three nations post-1950. Even in those nations, it has merely escaped falsification. There are other factors that may have been present among the affluent in 1950 and moved down to benefit the less affluent after that date, such as decent education or liberal parenting. Even if certain nations show a decline in IQ variance, that could well be due to factors other than nutrition. For example, large families show a wider range of IQ differences among their children than small families, presumably because parents are less able to give infants attention as the number of children increases. So a drop in family size can cause reduced IQ variance.

Some take the fact that height has increased in the twentieth century as a substitute for direct evidence (Lynn, 1989). After all, better nutrition must have caused height gains and if it increased height, why not IQ? However, the notion that height gains show that IQ was being raised by better nutrition is easily falsified. All we need is a period during which height gains occurred and during which IQ gains were not concentrated in the lower half of the IQ distribution. Martorell (1998) shows that height gains persisted in the Netherlands until children born about 1965. Yet, children born between 1934 and 1964 show massive Raven's-type gains throughout the whole range of IQs. French children gained in height until at least those born in 1965. Yet, children born between 1931 and 1956 show massive Raven's gains that were uniform up through the 90th percentile.

Norway has been cited as a nation in which the nutrition hypothesis is viable, thanks to greater gains in the lower half of the IQ distribution. Actually, it provides a decisive piece of evidence against the posited connection between height gains and IQ gains. Height gains have been larger in the upper half of the height distribution than in the lower half (Sundet, Barlaug, & Torjussen, 2004). This combination, greater height gains in the upper half of the distribution, greater IQ gain in the lower, falsifies the posited causal hypothesis: greater nutritional gains among the less affluent as a common cause of both greater height and IQ gains. US data are equally damning. Height gains occurred until children born about 1952. Fortunately, a combination of Wechsler and Stanford–Binet data gives the rate of IQ gains before and after that date, that is, from about 1931 to 1952 and from 1952 to 2002. The rate of gain is virtually constant (at 0.325 points per year) throughout the whole period – the cessation of the height gains makes no difference whatsoever (Flynn, 1984a, Table 2;

Flynn & Weiss, in press). It is worth noting that there is no evidence that the ratio of brain size to height increased in the twentieth century.

Finally, the twin studies pose a dilemma for those who believe that early childhood nutrition has sizable effects on IQ. The differences in nutrition would be primarily between middle-class and poor families. Children who went to school with a better brain due to good nutrition would have the same advantage as those with a better brain due to good genes. By adulthood, the impact of their better nutrition would be multiplied so that it accounted for a significant proportion of IQ differences or variance. Yet, the twin studies show that family environment fades away to virtually nothing by adulthood (Jensen, 1998). I can see no solution to this dilemma.

A personal confession

The methodological mistake that impeded the solution of our paradoxes does me no credit. I was inhibited by using a wrong-headed method to assess the potency of environmental factors, namely, the method of weighting factors from two static contexts so as to measure the effects of dynamic processes over time. This method made every possible environmental factor look too feeble to be taken seriously and, therefore, left me at a loss. I knew that massive IQ gains had to be environmental in origin, but no collection of environmental causes seemed to have the potency to match such huge effects.

A hypothetical example will expose the mistake. Over thirty years, a nation enjoys an IQ gain of 20 points and an SES gain such that the top 75 percent in 1980 matches the top 50 percent of 1950. To calculate the impact of rising affluence on IQ gains, I used data that differentiated the top and lower halves of the population for IQ. These suggested a difference of about 12 IQ points. So if 25 percent had moved from the bottom to the top half,

Box 10

The details of the calculation run as follows:

(1) 1950 – The top 50 percent of an IQ curve has a mean of 112. Assuming a correlation between SES and IQ of 0.50, the top 50 percent in SES would have a mean IQ of 106. The bottom 50 percent would have a mean of 94.
(2) 1980 – Weighting for the fact that the top 75 percent matches the SES of the top 50 percent of 1950: $106 \times 75 = 7{,}950$. Weighting for the fact that the bottom 25 percent matches the SES of the bottom 50 percent of 1950: $94 \times 25 = 2{,}350$.
(3) Result: $7{,}950 + 2{,}350 = 10{,}300$ and that divided by 100 equals 103. So SES seems to explain only 3 points of the 20-point IQ gain.

the gain from one generation to another would be only 3 IQ points and account for only a fragment of the 20-point gain (see Box 10).

This inappropriate method was the one I used to dismiss the role of rising SES as an explanation of massive IQ gains in the Netherlands between 1952 and 1982 (Flynn, 1987). Apologies to all misled thereby. The seductive appeal of this method must have been that it offered nice neat calculations. Because I had always known (and often said) that the significance of SES within a generation is completely different from its significance between generations. Within generations, competition for wealth and status is the major factor that correlates IQ and SES. Why should IQ differentials that are a product of a status competition be in any way indicative of IQ differentials between generations?

If we think of a rise in SES as a proxy for rising affluence, the estimate that it was responsible for a gain of only 3 IQ points between generations is ludicrous. The most profound result of the industrial revolution since 1950 is affluence. The post-World War II economic boom did much to weaken the "depression psychology" of the 1930s. Preoccupation with practical concerns like earning a living diminished, so that abstract problems were no longer seen as a trivial distraction from the real business of life. Leisure no longer exhausted by recuperation from the demands of work was a factor that pushed leisure activities toward hobbies (like chess and bridge) and conversation and video games that exercise the mind. The number of jobs emphasizing manipulation of symbols or abstractions and on-the-spot problem solving increased. Middle-class mores and aspirations reduced family size.

Tuddenham (1948) used the weighting method to measure the impact of schooling gains on IQ gains between 1917 and 1943. He notes that the mean number of years of schooling had risen from eight to ten years and that weighting the 1917 sample to match the 1943 sample for schooling eliminated half of the score difference. He was lucky. Schooling was so important that weighting for years of schooling captured much of its impact. To be fair, Tuddenham notes that quality of schooling may have risen and that quantitative measures may underestimate its full impact. Let us build on this remark by giving a dynamic account.

Between 1917 and 1943, society greatly intensified its demand for school-taught cognitive skills. Each student became surrounded by fellow students who were more motivated and competent, better students become better teachers for the next cohort of students, parents become more serious about schooling and homework, the lengths of the school day and school year tend to increase. Only a fragment of this is captured by adding on to the 1917 sample the benefit of an extra two years of schooling of the kind that existed in their day. Or, conversely, reducing the 1943 sample to match the eight years of schooling of the earlier sample would not mean that both samples are benefiting from eight years of the same kind of school experience.

The same point can be made about other trends, for example, urbanization. Flieller, Saintigny, and Schaeffer (1986) note that the shift from rural to urban does not seem to account for much of French IQ gains. To test this, I did the usual weighting calculations for a shift from rural to urban and found almost nil effect. Geographical IQ differences at any given time also reflect a kind of competition: a competition for desirable space, that is, going to the city for better jobs or fleeing the inner city because of crime. And these shifts lead to either positive or negative IQ differences. But these differences miss everything important that was happening in rural communities over time. And they miss what was happening in urban communities. Industrialization and growing affluence meant greater sophistication not only within cities but also within rural areas that were no longer isolated thanks to travel and the media.

Recently, Herrnstein and Murray (1994, pp. 363–368) used the weighting method to estimate the effects of an IQ shift of 3 points from one time to another. All sorts of social problems from illegitimacy to crime were shown to diminish. These predictions, if that is what they were, tell us nothing whatsoever about what would actually happen. It all depends on what would cause the IQ shift and what other effects that cause might have. It might be that IQ drops 3 points because a larger number of affluent middle-class children prefer wandering around shopping malls to profiting from schooling and that the effects on crime and illegitimacy are nil. It might be that a larger number of children are raised in solo-parent homes and that such an environment lowers IQ by 3 points. Then the enhanced social problem would have caused the IQ loss and not the reverse.

The authors say that the exercise assumes that everything else but IQ remains constant; and that things would be more complicated in the real world. This amounts to saying that if you ignore all of the important dynamic processes, something that is relatively unimportant may loom large. They note only one dynamic process: over perhaps ninety years, people with less education have had marginally more children than people with more education. The fear is that poor genes for IQ will multiply and that there will be a gradual decline in average brain quality. That is not desirable, but even so, there is no reason to believe that the resulting population would have brains too limited to meet social demands.

If tolerance for cognitively demanding school environments diminishes, it would be premature to assign this to the advent of physiological limitations. A thousand sociological hypotheses are equally plausible to explain why people or, more precisely, why American whites rebel against more difficult classroom-subject material, a longer school day, more homework, less leisure, and so forth. Our brains as presently constructed probably have much excess capacity ready to be used if needed. That was certainly the case in 1900.

Psychology and sociology

The reason it took me so long to think intelligently about massive IQ gains over time was unused brain capacity. My mind was so compartmentalized, I ignored everything I knew from another discipline, namely, sociology. As Schooler says (1998, p. 72), the first thing you learn is that SES and rural residence and years of schooling are not personal traits that are relatively fixed like fingerprints, but rather social creations that may change as dramatically over time as the motor car you drive.

No one should do psychology without some sociological sophistication. Hegel once said that to really understand the least facet of the universe we must know the whole. Pity the poor social scientist. Before we know anything about human behavior, we must know something about virtually every one of the human sciences.

6   IQ gains can kill

> These death sentences are cruel and unusual in the same
> way that being struck by lightning is cruel and unusual . . .
> (T)he Eighth and Fourteenth Amendments cannot tolerate
> the infliction of a sentence of death under legal systems that
> permit this unique penalty to be so wantonly and so freakishly
> imposed.
>
> (Justice Stewart in *Furman* v. *Georgia*, 1972)

Some people are peculiar in the sense that they are less interested
in the advancement of knowledge than in practical matters.
Massive IQ gains over time have practical relevance because they
expose mistakes in measuring IQ. These mistakes are costly
because they deceive us about causes and even deceive us into
putting people to death who ought to be exempt. The root cause of
all of these unfortunate consequences is scoring against "obsolete
norms."

Obsolete norms

An IQ score is only as valid as the test the person takes,
and the test is only as valid as the standardization sample on
which it is normed. When someone is assigned an IQ of 100 that
means that their performance on a particular test was exactly
average or at the 50th percentile. And the score is accurate only if
the person is being compared to a representative sample of his
or her peers, for example, a representative sample of American
14-year-olds tested at exactly the same time. The reason the test

must have been normed recently is the existence of massive IQ gains over time.

For the Wechsler (WISC and WAIS) and the Stanford–Binet IQ tests, the best rule of thumb is that Full Scale IQ gains have been proceeding at a rate of 0.30 points per year ever since 1947. This rate is based on comparisons of all of the Wechsler and Stanford–Binet tests used in recent years (see Box 11). It means that for every year that passes between when an IQ test was normed, that is, when its standardization sample was tested, and when subjects are tested, obsolescence has inflated their IQs by 0.30 points. For example, if you took the WISC (normed in 1947–1948) in 1977–1978, you would get an unearned bonus of 9 IQ points (30 years × 0.30). Even though you might be dead average, you would be scored at 109 thanks to obsolete norms thirty years out of date. After all, IQ gains over time mean that as we go back into the past, representative samples of Americans perform worse and worse. In this case, you are not being compared to your peers, the 14-years-olds of the late 1970s, but to a much lower-scoring group, the 14-year-olds of the late 1940s. Your score of 109 against the old norms makes you appear above average, but you are actually no better than average and deserve an IQ of 100.

The easiest way to correct your score, of course, is to deduct the proper number of points: 0.30 points for every year that lapses between when the test was normed and when you took it. In this case, we would deduct 9 points and you would get a corrected and accurate IQ score of 100. Failure to adjust the scores is to take flight from reality. Suppose you are coaching an athlete who aspires to qualify for the Olympic high jump. He jumps 6 feet 6 inches and you assure him that he will qualify. He replies: "But that was the standard in 1975. Since then, performances have improved and today I have to jump 7 feet to qualify. You are judging my performance in terms of the norms of yesterday rather than today." He would do well to hire a new coach.

Box 11

Below are the results all recent pairs of tests (see Table 3 in Appendix 1 for full data and the full names of the tests).

> WISC-R (1972) and WAIS-R (1978): rate of +0.150 points per year
>
> SB-LM (1972) and SB-4 (1985): rate of +0.166 points per year
>
> WISC-R (1972) and SB-4 (1985): rate of +0.227 points per year
>
> WISC-R (1972) and WISC-III (1989): rate of +0.312 points per year
>
> WAIS-R (1978) and SB-4 (1985): rate of +0.489 points per year
>
> WAIS-R (1978) and WAIS-III (1995): rate of +0.171 points per year
>
> SB-4 (1985) and SB-5 (2001): rate of +0.173 points per year
>
> WISC-III (1989) and WAIS-III (1995): rate of –0.117 points per year
>
> WISC-III (1989) and SB-5 (2001): rate of 0.417 points per year
>
> WISC-III (1989) and WISC-III/IV (2001.75): rate of + 0.332 points per year
>
> WAIS-III (1995) and SB-5 (2001): rate of +0.917 points per year
>
> WAIS-III (1995) and WISC-IV (2001.75): rate of +0.459 points per year
>
> **AVERAGE OF THE 12**: rate of +0.308 points per year or about 0.30.

Unless corrected, obsolete norms deceive. We begin with a mixture of the ridiculous and the horrible. In America, achievement tests have shown gains over time for young children. Scoring children against obsolete norms created an absurd situation in which every one of America's fifty states claimed that their schoolchildren were above the national average (Cannell, 1998). School officials and parents were gratified.

In 1995, the Press Trust of India distributed extracts from a report by A. Gupta, N. K. Sanghi, R. Sharma, and D. C. Jam concerning child laborers in India who were getting no schooling (Reuters, 1995). They put their mean IQ at 130. First, there is the sheer stupidity of it. Presumably, the test was not normed in India (it is hardly possible that non-elite children in India were 30 points above the average child in India). An IQ of 130 puts you at the 98th percentile, so these children were supposed to be better than practically all of the children in some other nation like America. Clearly, they had found a test whose norms were radically obsolete. Taking the IQs at face value, they recommended that a ban on child labor (widely flouted) should be applied only to dangerous jobs (they had also found that child laborers in general suffered no unusual physical disabilities; see Box 12). They tested a sample of children in school

---

Box 12

In the early nineteenth century, children aged 7 crawled through British coal mines dragging carts after them. A debate in the House of Lords records the view that while this might be bad for upper-class children, working-class children were a different breed. More difficult to defend was the practice of cutting niches into the wall where children aged 4 sat in the dark all day, opening and closing the ventilation traps. Mercifully, they sometimes dropped off to sleep and fell into the machinery. It is a pity that no one could measure their IQs (Krugman, 1994).

---

and put their average IQ at 120. Well, there are samples and samples. If Indian schools really cost their pupils 10 IQ points, it is time to move in with the machine guns and tanks, level the buildings, and salt the ruins.

Obsolete norms and Chinese Americans

Forty years ago, Nathaniel Weyl (1966, 1969) called Chinese Americans part of "the American natural aristocracy." Chinese Americans had three to five times their proportionate share of college faculty, architects, scientists, school teachers, engineers, and physicians, and fell behind whites only where political connections count – lawyers and judges – and in sub-professions like nursing and the clergy. Weyl gave a scenario for the positive selection of Chinese for intelligence: competitive exams throughout Chinese history had created an intellectual elite who had plural wives and more offspring.

The children of Weyl's subjects were born in the 1970s and 1980s. In 1985, the upper 70 percent of Asian 18-year-olds took the Scholastic Aptitude Test (SAT) and matched the upper 27 percent of whites, lower on the verbal test but higher on the mathematics test (ETS, 1985, 1988). Between 1981 and 1987, Asian American high-school students were much over-represented among winners of National Merit Scholarships, US Presidential Scholarships, Arts Recognition and Talent Search scholars, and Westinghouse Science Talent Search scholars. This last, America's most prestigious high-school science competition, had twenty Asian winners out of the seventy chosen over those seven years, indeed, in 1986, the top five winners were all Asian Americans.

The number of Asian Americans at prestige universities was staggering. Asian Americans were just over 2 percent of the population, and yet, the 1984 entering class had 9 percent Asians at Princeton, 11 percent at Harvard and Stanford, 19 percent at the California Institute of Technology and Berkeley. By 1987, the percentages were even higher: 14 percent at Harvard, 16 percent at Stanford, 20 percent at the Massachusetts Institute of Technology, 21 percent at Cal Tech, 25 percent at Berkeley, and this despite accusations that admissions quotas had been introduced to limit their numbers. The famed Juilliard School of Music has consistently had a student body 25 percent Asian. These high achievers were not all Chinese, of course, but all the evidence indicated that Chinese Americans as a subgroup of the Asian American community punched above their weight (Flynn, 1991a).

The obvious explanation of why Asian Americans did so well was that they were smarter; and this view seemed vindicated by Vernon's great book, *The abilities and achievements of Orientals in North America*, which was published in 1982. Vernon was impressed by recent studies that put Chinese American verbal IQ at 97, or little below the white average, and put their non-verbal IQ at 110 or well above the white average. It is clear that the recent studies Vernon has in mind are these: Jensen's testing of children from San Francisco's Chinatown, done in 1975, which gave them a verbal IQ of 97 and a non-verbal IQ of 110 on the Lorge–Thorndike Intelligence Test; and a study by Jensen and Inouye of children in the Berkeley, California, public schools which gave Oriental children (more Chinese than Japanese) very high Lorge–Thorndike IQs. Vernon discounted the Berkeley results somewhat, due to the elite character of the school district, but believed that they reinforced the Chinatown results.

My suspicions were aroused by the fact that as late as 1965, the Coleman Report had put Chinese and Japanese non-verbal IQ at 100, or no higher than whites. I knew from personal correspondence with Jensen that the Berkeley study had actually been done in 1968 and wondered if Vernon had thought it done circa 1980. A 10-point rise in Chinese non-verbal IQ (from 100 to 110) between 1965 and 1980 was unlikely, but such a rise between 1965 and 1968 was quite incredible. Moreover, when the elite Chinese of Berkeley were compared to the elite whites of Berkeley, the Chinese actually had somewhat lower IQs. And the IQ values for both races looked odd: for example, Berkeley whites had 118 for verbal IQ and 120 for non-verbal IQ. No school district in America should have an average IQ that high, however elite it might be.

I began to suspect that the Berkeley IQs had been inflated by the fact that the Lorge–Thorndike test norms were obsolete. If the test had been normed not in 1968, when the children were tested, but say back in 1953, the Berkeley children were being scored against a sample fifteen years out of date, not a representative sample of contemporary children. And this cast doubt on the results of the Chinatown study: if Berkeley children tested in 1968 had inflated IQs because of obsolete Lorge–Thorndike norms, the Chinatown children of 1975 would have IQs even more inflated.

Therefore, I felt I had good reason to isolate the Chinese Americans who began to mature in the 1970s and 1980s and see what a full review of the data on their IQs would show. After all, if Vernon was mistaken, we needed a whole new pair of spectacles. High IQ and high achievement seemed to reinforce one another as evidence of the superior intelligence of Chinese Americans. But if their mean IQ was no higher than whites, or even below whites, then the brute facts would dictate that non-IQ factors have a potent role for group achievement. A problem that seemed rather humdrum (they do so well because they are smarter) suddenly posed a challenge to the intellect.

A review of sixteen studies done from 1938 to 1985 and involving 11,373 subjects showed that my suspicions were correct. When IQs were adjusted against norms set by contemporary white controls, the means fell to no higher than 97 for verbal IQ (here Vernon had been correct) and 100 for non-verbal IQ, the latter no higher than whites. Some of these studies lumped together both Chinese and Japanese Americans, but nine studies that distinguished them (with about 2,800 Chinese subjects and 3,600

Japanese) showed that the two groups were virtually identical. The best data were from the Coleman Report, which tested an excellent sample of high-school seniors (aged 17) in 1965. I felt that the way to tell the true story of Chinese American achievement was to follow the graduating class of 1966 from birth to the 1980 census, by which time they were full-fledged adults (Flynn, 1991a, Tables 4.1 and 4.2).

The class of 1966

The Chinese American members of the class of 1966 were born circa 1948 and raised in homes roughly equivalent to whites in terms of socio-economic status. About 65 percent were native born and 35 percent foreign born. In 1980, fourteen years after graduation, the Chinese native and foreign born did not differ significantly for achievement as measured by occupational status.

In grade school, these Chinese Americans had lower verbal IQs than whites and no higher non-verbal IQs, although they were more precocious on tests of map skills and figure copying. When matched with whites for IQ, they outperformed them on achievement tests by a small margin, equivalent to about 2 IQ points, doing better in English than mathematics, particularly well in spelling. Very few of them were scholastically retarded and this persisted into high school. Only 7 percent of them ever lagged a grade or more behind their age group as compared to 12 percent of whites.

By high school, their over-performance on achievement tests had become highly significant, equivalent to about 5 IQ points, and the balance between subjects had altered. When matched with whites for non-verbal IQ, they outperformed whites on mathematics tests by 6 points; when matched for verbal IQ, on English tests by 3 or 4 points. Their over-performance was higher on tests of school-taught subjects than cognitive tests and highest of all in advanced mathematics; indeed, tests of analytic geometry and calculus showed huge over-performances of up to 15 points. When matched with whites for IQ, they did better in terms of high-school grades than on the typical achievement test, over-performing by the equivalent of at least 7 IQ points. Few dropped out of high school and some of these later returned to earn their diploma. Eventually 95 percent would graduate as compared to just under 89 percent of whites.

During their senior year of high school, the Coleman Report confirmed that the class of 1966 had lower IQs than their white counterparts: they had a verbal IQ of 97 and a non-verbal IQ of 100. During their junior and senior years, at least 50 percent took the Scholastic Aptitude Test (SAT) while the figure for whites was less than 30 percent. This 5 to 3 ratio was very close to that which they would later achieve in attaining high-status occupations. Despite being much less highly selected than white SAT candidates, they were only 1.3 points below whites overall, being slightly superior on the SAT mathematics, suffering from a deficit on the SAT verbal. They could concede whites 4.5 IQ points and yet match them on the SAT and concede them almost 7 IQ points and yet match them for high-school grades.

This meant that they could secure entry to the same universities as whites despite lower IQs. At Berkeley in the fall of 1966, native-born Chinese entrants had an IQ threshold 7 points below whites. Despite this, they were as successful at university as whites. Their final year found them contemplating graduate study with a ratio compared to whites equal to the 5 to 3 ratio they had enjoyed when contemplating undergraduate study. On the Graduate Record Examination (GRE) and admissions tests for medical, law, and business schools, they matched or bettered their performance of four years earlier. Between the SAT and these graduate tests, they lowered their deficit vis-à-vis whites from 1.3 points to less than one.

In 1980, when 32 years of age, the Chinese members of the class of 1966 had 55 percent of their number in managerial, professional, or technical occupations, while their white contemporaries had only 34 percent. This meant that Chinese Americans had mimicked a subgroup of the white population with a mean IQ of almost 120, which was 21 points above their actual mean. In 1980, the Chinese members of the class had incomes 20 percent above their white contemporaries.

The explanation of these massive IQ/occupational achievement gaps lay in certain ethnic differences. Chinese Americans could qualify for high-status occupations with an IQ threshold about 7 points below the white threshold, which gave them a pool of potential achievers larger than their mean IQ would have led one to expect. Moreover, they capitalized on that pool with greater efficiency, that is, 78 percent of Chinese capable of attaining managerial, professional, or technical occupations did so. Whites capitalized on only 60 percent of their available pool of talent. This ends our account of the history of the class of 1966 (Flynn, 1991a, Tables 5.1 and 5.8).

As to the kind of ethnic differences that advantage Chinese Americans, their parents surround them with a childhood environment more cognitively demanding than that enjoyed by white Americans. However, recall that parents cannot endow their children with a permanent advantage unless they effect a change that makes them atypical of the larger society, that is, they must create within their minds a desire for cognitive challenge and within their hearts a passion for educational achievement. That Chinese American parents can do this is signaled by the proclivity of their children to capitalize on opportunities to achieve high occupational status. If an Irish lad qualifies for an elite university and his fiancée wants him to stay at home, he may do so. A Chinese youth is likely to get a new fiancée.

The class of 1966 is now almost sixty years old, and today, we know something about their children. Richard Lynn (in press)

Box 13

The values I have assigned to various ages were derived from the studies listed below. Most of the samples were not purely Chinese but East Asians, which include Japanese and Koreans as well. However, all existent data show results for these groups to be much the same.

(1) 108.6 for age 6: the weighted average of the results from Rushton (1997), 63 subjects aged 7, and French (2001), 18 subjects median age 5.5.

(2) 104 at age 10.5: the weighted average of Jensen and Wang (1994), 155 subjects aged 10, and Lynn (1996b), 48 subjects median age 11.5.

(3) 103 at age 18: the result from Herrnstein and Murray (1994), 42 subjects median age 18.

---

has collected fascinating IQ data for samples tested since 1986. These vary in age and year of testing. However, I am going to refer to them as the class of 1990 because that was the year in which a group with 18 as its median age was tested and it is the only adult sample. With white IQ set at 100, the class of 1990 had a mean IQ of 108.6 at age 6, falling to 104 at age 10.5, and falling to 103 at age 18 (see Box 13).

This pattern is exactly what the Dickens/Flynn model would predict. The class of 1966 was raised in homes of only average socio-economic status but, thanks to their achievements, they became largely upper class and could provide their own preschool children with a cognitive environment even more enriched than the one they enjoyed. Their preschool children attained a mean IQ almost 9 points above the white average. However, much of that advantage was lost when school began to dilute parental influence and it declined further to a 3-IQ-point advantage as they entered adulthood.

Although the numbers from recent studies are not large enough for strong inference, Chinese American environmental progress over the last half-century makes 103 a reasonable value. I believe that the IQ gap between the class of 1966 and the class of 1990 should be put at only 3 points. About 35 percent of the former were foreign born and, therefore, the non-verbal value of 100 is a better estimate of their real IQ than the verbal value of 97. The fact that Chinese Americans are now 3 points above white Americans is a good measure of the cognitive advantage conferred by their distinctive subculture. There is every reason to believe that the class of 1990 has internalized the goal of seeking out cognitive challenge more than most. We know that they have disproportionately entered elite universities and when the census of 2010 appears, it will be surprising if it does not show them disproportionately concentrated in cognitively demanding occupations.

The alternative to my emphasis on a distinctive subculture and incentive system, of course, is to argue that Chinese Americans have a genic IQ of 103 and are merely accessing superior environments of matching quality. This overlooks an inconvenient fact: they access environments whose cognitive complexity is above any value they have ever recorded for IQ and they maintain that environmental "surplus" at least to retirement. If those environments make any contribution at all, their genic IQ should be close to 100 and on a par with whites.

Setting their genes aside, one thing is clear. Chinese Americans are an ethnic group for whom high achievement preceded high IQ rather than the reverse. It is not easy to view the history of their achievements without emotion. Nothing I have said diminishes these people, unless someone believes that achievement with average IQ is less worthy than achievement with high IQ. Only when we correct for the obsolete norms that inflated their IQs can we fully appreciate what they have accomplished. There is an irony in the fact that they overcame bias wherever they encountered it at a time when they did not excel on the putatively unbiased IQ test.

Obsolete norms and American blacks

By 2002, the mean IQ of black American children aged 4 had risen to 95.4. This puts them less than 5 points below white 4-year-olds at 100. However, by the age of 24, blacks lose fully 12 points and sink to 83.4, almost 17 points below whites. In other words, they lose 0.60 points per year as they age. The cause of this loss demands urgent study. But, until recently, the fact that it occurs has been obscured by obsolete norms in that blacks have been making IQ gains over time at a rate of 0.45 IQ points per year (Dickens & Flynn, 2006).

Imagine using a test normed in 2000 to test a group of black children as they age. In 2000, tested at the age of 4, there is no obsolescence; but in 2001 at age 5, their IQs are inflated by one year of obsolescence, and in 2002 at age 6, they are inflated by two years of obsolescence. Clearly the inflation they enjoy from obsolescence will cancel out most of their loss with age, that is, with each passing year they gain 0.45 points and lose 0.60 points. Over any period of say four years (testing them yearly), their unadjusted IQs will drop hardly at all. It is only when you adjust

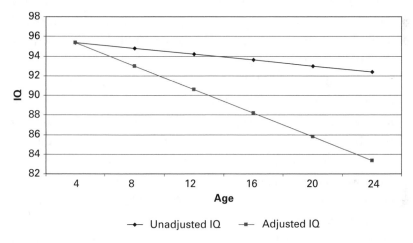

Figure 3 With white IQ fixed at 100, black children lose ground on whites as they age (adjusted IQs); this is obscured by obsolescence (unadjusted IQs).

their scores for obsolete norms that the ground lost with age becomes apparent (see Figure 3).

Obsolete norms and interventions

Obsolete norms can either deflate or inflate our estimate of how much interventions have raised IQs, but the cases in which they inflate scores usually have the more serious consequences. The Milwaukee Project was one of the most radical interventions ever attempted. Preschool children were not only taken away from their homes each day to educational centers staffed by sub-professionals but also efforts were made to upgrade their home environment by finding their mothers employment. In 1972, when first results showed that these ghetto black children had a mean IQ of over 120, the general reaction was to take the scores at face value (Clarke, 1973; Mussen, Conger, & Kagan, 1974). This was actually the product of using the Stanford–Binet, which had been normed in 1932 and was, therefore, forty years obsolescent. Fortunately, the investigators used a control group to check the effects of the intervention, so they were much more guarded. By the time they published their account in book form, the problem of IQs inflated by obsolete norms was known and they adjusted their results accordingly (Garber, 1988).

Transferring a child from its birth parents into an adoptive home is perhaps the most radical kind of environmental intervention. Skodak and Skeels (1949) is considered the classic adoption study because it gave IQ scores for both the adopted children and their biological mothers. The reported results proclaimed the good news that adoption had allowed these children to outscore their mothers by 20 IQ points or more. In fact, at least one-third of the children's advantage was a result of using the 1916 Stanford–Binet whose norms were both suspect and obsolete. The true IQ advantage of the adopted children over their biological mothers was somewhere between 10 and 13 points (Flynn, 1993b).

In New Zealand, some years ago, prisoners were thought to have above average IQs (Reid & Gilmore, 1988). This was surprising. Was the cognitive environment of New Zealand prisons so good that being jailed amounted to a favorable environmental intervention? (Fortunately, those who think prisoners are coddled did not notice the finding.) Could it be that having better genes for intelligence predisposed one for criminality? The test used, of course, was radically obsolete.

Classifying people as mentally retarded

The American Association on Mental Retardation has recently altered its name to the American Association on Intellectual and Developmental Disabilities. However, since the literature I will cite was published under the rubric AAMR, I will use the old name herein. Its criteria for classifying people as mentally retarded recommends an IQ score of approximately 70 to 75 but stresses that scores can be overridden by poor adaptive behavior as diagnosed by clinical psychologists (AAMR, 2002, p. 58). If IQ scores are significant because they usually signal maladaptive behavior, then IQ gains over time pose a fundamental question. People in the retardate score range have gained like everybody else. Therefore, we face a familiar paradox. If IQ gains over time are intelligence gains, those at low IQ levels have progressed to the point where hardly any of them are really mentally retarded. On the other hand, if people at low IQ levels have not progressed to the point at which they can cope with the real world, IQ gains over time must be mere artifacts.

My answer to this paradox has already been implied. I think IQ gains are significant even though they have little to do with improved competence to cope with the concrete world of everyday life. People have been fully motivated to try to deal with that world ever since human beings evolved. Most rural Americans in the nineteenth century showed they could learn to use dogs to hunt rabbits but there was a small minority, about 2 percent, who just could not do so.

I see no reason to think that anything has changed. About 2 percent of people today cannot learn to manage for themselves, for example, they cannot be trusted to drive a car or mind someone else's children. One might argue that the modern world is such that even basic skills are more complex than in the nineteenth century. I am skeptical. Driving is not more complicated than hunting and the skills you really need to cope on a minimal level are much the same: remembering to do things on time, having basic literacy and numeracy (so you can shop and make change), having the sense not to let other people lead you into obvious mischief, and so forth. We do not classify people as MR today because they cannot fill out complex tax forms.

IQ gains over time are significant because they mean enhanced ability to do things that lie well beyond adaptive behavior in the context of concrete reality. They mean innovative thinking in professional work roles, being comfortable with the hypothetical when it is used to pose abstract or moral problems, and so forth. Low-IQ subjects get a few more items right on IQ tests today for the same reason average people get a lot more items right. Compared to the mentally retarded of the past, they get much more formal schooling. When confronted with a simple Similarities item, such as how are hammers and spades alike, they are much more likely to say that they are both tools than to say you hit nails with one and dig with the other.

There is a test that measures competency in everyday life called the Vineland Adaptive Behavior Scales. For the first time, we can check whether these skills rose during a period of rapid IQ gains. From the 1989 standardization of the WISC-III on a representative sample of American children at that time to the 2002 standardization of the WISC-IV, there was an IQ gain of over 4 IQ points (look back to that pair of tests in Box 11). The Vineland was standardized on children aged 7 to 18 in both 1984 and 2005

(Vineland, 2006). A group of today's children took both tests and actually found the 1984 norms more difficult to meet than current norms. They received an overall Adaptive Behavior Composite of only 95.0 on the old test and one of 98.4 on the new test (SD = 15). This seems to indicate that American schoolchildren actually lost 3.4 points in terms of adaptive behavior since 1984.

However, their scores on the Communication and Socialization subtests were similar on the two versions. The lost ground was almost entirely on the Daily Living Skills subtest. The 1984 version of that subtest contains obsolete skills that would deflate the scores of contemporary children (items such as "sews or hems clothes," "makes own bed," and "uses a pay telephone"). The most judicious conclusion is that American children have marked time during a period in which they made large IQ gains. Which is to say that IQ gains over time do not mean that fewer and fewer children find it difficult to cope with everyday life.

We return to the problems posed by obsolete norms. An IQ of 70 or below shows that a child is in the bottom 2 percent or, as we now know, it shows that if the norms are current. If they are thirty years obsolete, the child gets a bonus of 9 points and a child whose true IQ is 65 will be credited with a score of 74. Since IQ tests sometimes wait twenty-five years to be renormed, and since school psychologists often use up their stock of old tests even after a new one has appeared, the percentage of American children that were eligible to be classified as MR has fluctuated wildly. Flynn (2000c) calculated a worse-case scenario taking into account obsolescence, plus the fact that gains may have been slightly greater at the level of MR, plus the fact that the criterion of MR was altered from norms based on white subjects only to those based on all races. Between 1947 and 1999, the proportion eligible to be classified as MR fluctuated from 1 in 23 (4.35 percent) to 1 in 213 (0.47 percent); and this assumes that no one used up copies of an obsolete test.

Over the last half century, the target percentage of about 2 percent has been attained only fleetingly and then only by accident. Whether a child's IQ score indicated he or she should be classified as MR was a lottery. If you happened to be tested just before an obsolete test was about to be renormed, you got bonus points that might save you from being classified as MR; if you happened to take a test that had just been renormed, you did not get the bonus points. If you were tested both before and after the renorming, your recorded IQ showed a dramatic drop. This spurious IQ loss might determine your fate, that is, get you reclassified as MR particularly if you had switched schools.

Kanaya, Scullin, and Ceci (2003) point out how important it is to get MR classifications correct. Each year 2 million children are tested for special education, including MR services, and in a given school year over 600,000 actually receive MR services. If those with inflated IQs, thanks to obsolete norms, are not classified as MR, the government saves millions of dollars because it does not have to provide special services. But children do not get the help they need. Adults who are classified as MR are eligible for social security disability benefits and are ineligible for military service. If the military did not update their norms, they would enlist thousands of people who, at least in their opinion, lack the ability to make correct decisions on the battlefield. The losses in money and lives are potentially huge.

Although the problem of obsolete norms has been public since 1984, school psychologists have been slow to recognize the problems posed when a new IQ test replaces an older one. Kanaya et al. found that after the WISC-III was published in 1991, there was an immediate rise in the number of children being classified as MR. Thanks to IQ gains over time, children in the retardate range who took the new test were averaging 5.6 IQ points lower than those who were still taking the old test. If IQ were the sole criterion of MR, and if everyone used the new WISC-III as soon as it was available, this would raise the number classified as MR from less than 1 percent (0.89) in 1990 to almost 2 percent (1.97) in 1991, that is, there would be an abrupt doubling of the number overnight.

The immediate effect was not quite that dramatic. Kenaya *et al.* selected a large, economically and geographically diverse sample of students tested for special education. They found that not all school psychologists were using the new test. In 1991, 88 percent of students were still being given the old WISC-R. In 1992, this dropped to 41 percent, but even in 1995, the old test was still in use. However, the new test was beginning to make a difference. Those psychologists who first tested a child on the WISC-R and then retested using the WISC-III were twice as likely to submit a recommendation of MR, when compared to those who retested using the same test. Those who had only the new lower WISC-III score were even more likely to use the label MR. Between 1991 and 1995, thousands and thousands of children did or did not receive an MR diagnosis simply because of the test they took. In passing, note that by 1996, the WISC-III was itself seven years obsolete and inflating IQs by 2 points.

What would we predict for America as a whole based on the above timetable? Focusing on the last twenty-five years, we would predict that as the WISC-R norms became more and more obsolete as the 1980s progressed, the number classified as MR would drop. And that after the new WISC-III was published, the mid 1990s would usher in an upward trend.

Scullin (in press) collected data from all fifty states plus Washington, DC, to trace trends concerning the percentage of students enrolled in MR programs. He found that a steady and general decline during the 1980s turned into an increase in the mid 1990s in forty-three states and Washington, DC. By 1993, MR rates were only 62 percent of the rate for 1981. But by 1999, they had rebounded to 80 percent of the 1981 rate. We would have predicted that by 1999, the rate would be 100 percent of the 1981 rate. In 1999, the WISC-III norms were ten years out of date, exactly the same as the ten-year-old WISC-R norms in 1982. The reason that MR reached only 80 percent of its old level was that the new test was swimming against a tide. The diagnosis of learning disabled was replacing mentally retarded, thanks in part to the reluctance of school districts to assign the latter label, particularly to minority children.

The label may be new but "learning disabled" is also subject to the havoc wreaked by obsolete norms. The WISC-III manual notes that children with learning disabilities or reading disorders tend to do poorly on the four subtests of Arithmetic, Information, Coding, and Digit Span, that is, they have what is called an AICD profile (Wechsler, 1992, pp. 212–213). Getting your lowest scores on three of the four constitutes a partial AICD profile. The WISC-IV technical manual says that low scores on Arithmetic, Information, Vocabulary, and Letter–Number Sequencing characterize reading disability; and that low scores on Arithmetic, Information, and Comprehension go with expressive language disorder (Psychological Corporation, 2003, pp. 79–82).

Trends over time reveal that all of the above subtests except Coding and Comprehension have shown virtually nil gains over time with Letter–Number sequencing unknown because it is a new subtest (Flynn, 2006a, Table 1). It is huge gains on all of the other subtests that cause massive Full Scale IQ gains. In other words, after the WISC-III's norms became obsolete, perfectly normal children started to show a partial AICD profile. If they were typical of their cohort, they tended to score closer to the old norms on Arithmetic, Information, and Digit Span than on any other subtest. And after the WISC-IV's norms become obsolete (say around 2015), we have reason to believe that normal children will tend to look as if they have reading or language disorders. They will tend to do worse on Arithmetic, Information, and Vocabulary, and a bit below their average on Comprehension. If Letter–Number Sequencing follows suit, the problem will be compounded.

People at risk

The saddest consequence of obsolete norms is when they lead to the execution of someone who ought to be exempt from the death penalty. Today, those classified as MR are held not to be responsible for their actions. They usually need an IQ of 70 or below to be classified as such and if being scored against obsolete norms inflates their scores, they are at risk. Elsewhere, I have written a formal "brief" for attorneys with clients on death row (Flynn, 2006b). Here, I will only present the history of how the death penalty and IQ became intertwined.

In *Furman* v. *Georgia* (1972), on behalf of the US Supreme Court, Justice Stewart argued that the death penalty must be imposed with consistency and with due regard to the culpability of those who suffer its consequences. Thirty years later, in *Atkins* v. *Virginia* (2002), the Court held that the Eighth Amendment to the US Constitution forbids the death penalty for those who suffer from mental retardation. Subsequently, in *Walker* v. *True* (2005), the Fourth Circuit Court of Appeals held that in applying this standard, the "Flynn effect" had to be taken into account if it could be shown that it had affected the defendant's IQ score.

I have been approached by legal counsels in over a dozen post-conviction cases and have sworn eleven affidavits in five states: most were assessments of the IQ scores of defendants on death row; one was in support of a submission to the Florida Supreme Court advocating the relevance of the Flynn effect; another was a declaration requested by counsel for Walker when his case was returned to the Court of Appeals for decision. Similar submissions by others have been welcomed by the courts. In California, the court in *People* v. *Superior Court* (2005) said that the Flynn effect must be considered in determining a defendant's IQ and noted that this appeared to be generally accepted in the clinical field. Between 2004 and 2006, two Federal Courts of Appeal and eight courts in six states have discussed its relevance (see Box 14).

Box 14

Lawyers may be interested in a list of the relevant cases: *Black* v. *State*, 2005; *Bowling* v. *Commonwealth*, 2005; *Ex parte Murphy*, 2006; *In re Hicks*, 2004; *Myers* v. *State*, 2005; *People* v. *Superior Court*, 2005; *State* v. *Burke*, 2005; *State* v. *Murphy*, 2005; *Walker* v. *True*, 2005; *Walton* v. *Johnson*, 2005.

Most states that apply the death penalty have adopted a criterion for mental retardation that forces the defendant to evidence both poor adaptive functioning and an IQ score of 70 or below. It could be argued that this criterion is more stringent than that set by the American Association on Mental Retardation, which recommends a score of approximately 70 to 75. The AAMR also warns against too much reliance on IQ scores and advocates second-guessing IQ scores by using clinical judgment. The implication is that defendants who are classified as MR on behavioral criteria should not, in addition, have to produce a case based on IQ. However, the clinical judgments of prosecution and defense psychologists are almost always at variance and, therefore, defense attorneys feel constrained to make a case in terms of IQ in order to be taken seriously. Both the courts and the AAMR specify that MR should be apparent during the defendant's developmental period, that is, prior to the age of 18.

The question of poor adaptive functioning usually turns on sources of information such as interviews and examinations of the offender by school or clinical psychologists, medical histories, failure to qualify for a driver's license or hold anything but an unskilled job, and testimony by family and friends as to degree of suggestibility. As for case histories, they tend to fall into one of three categories:

(1) During the defendant's school years, there was at least one clear diagnosis of MR consequent on inability to cope, and a series of IQ scores at 70 or below.

(2) The defendant was evaluated at school and was not diagnosed as MR. However, there is reason to believe that the diagnosis was affected by the fact that IQ scores were inflated by obsolete norms.

(3) The defendant never received a formal diagnosis prior to age 18 and, therefore, prison diagnosis as an adult becomes crucial. Once again, IQ scores play a dual role: they must be interpreted properly to determine whether the defendant's IQ is really 70 or below; and they must be interpreted properly so that clinical judgment of adaptive behavior is not influenced, perhaps subconsciously, by an inflated IQ score.

There is also the possibility that a test will inflate IQ scores even though its norms are not obsolete. Presumably, judges will want to know if some IQ tests produce suspect scores in the sense that they rank people against a group that was unrepresentative even at the time it was selected. Imagine that a standardization sample was biased by including too many people with little education. Since the sample was substandard, it would be too easy to match the average performance and get an IQ of 100; and indeed, IQ scores all the way to the bottom would be inflated. This happens rarely but I will argue that one current IQ test stands out as an example.

The problem of adjusting IQ scores across nations and across different kinds of tests is complex. The rate of gain varies by country, for example, from America to Israel to Norway, and by test, for example, from matrices tests to purely verbal IQ tests (Flynn, 2006a). Those who deal with the scores of Americans on Wechsler and Stanford–Binet IQ tests are fortunate. As we saw in Chapter 2 (Figure 1), the rate of gain for Full Scale IQ has been roughly uniform at 0.30 points per year ever since 1947 and I will argue for adjusting scores using that rate. The comments of Trowbridge (April 2003) and Frumpkin (Fall 2003) on how to deal with expert testimony about IQ scores show that the formula of deducting 0.30 points per year is making headway at least among defense attorneys.

Special problems at low IQ levels

Recommending such a simple cure for obsolete norms assumes too much. It assumes that low-IQ subjects down at the level of 70 and below have been making IQ gains over time at much the same rate as average subjects; and it assumes that the only flaw in the tests we use is that their norms tend to become obsolete.

The courts prefer to trust IQ scores obtained when the defendant was at school and under the age of 18. But sometimes these are unavailable and often the results are ambiguous. Therefore, those who have committed capital crimes are usually tested post-conviction and since they are now adults, a recognized test with norms for adults must be used. The only ones available are the SB-5 and the WAIS-III, with the latter the most popular choice. Unfortunately, the WAIS-III has problems with its norms that go beyond obsolescence.

Remember the pattern that evidences IQ gains over time, namely, the older the test norms the easier it is to get a high score. Once again, the further we go back into the past, the worse the average performance that was used to norm the test; and the easier it is to exceed the average performance and get a score above 100. Let us imagine that, in 2000, the same group takes tests that were normed some years apart. They get an average IQ of 106 on Test A (normed 1980), 103 on Test B (normed 1990), and 100 on Test C (normed 2000). That would indicate a steady rate of gain of 0.30 points per year. Now imagine we insert a new test called B2 and that, wherever it appears, it disrupts the pattern. The group now averages 106 on Test A, 106 on Test B2, and 100 on Test C.

In other words, wherever Test B2 occurs as the later test in a combination, it reduces gains to nil (compare A and B2). And where it is the earlier test in a combination, it inflates gains to the improbable level of 6 points in only ten years (compare B2 and C). We would have a choice between concluding that the rate of gain was wildly eccentric and concluding that there was something wrong with the norms of Test B2. It consistently gives IQ gains well above or well below what we would expect. The obvious explanation is that its standardization sample was substandard even at the time it was selected. Perhaps high-IQ people were harder to recruit for the sample because they were too busy.

The WAIS-III behaves exactly like Test B2. As Figure 4 shows, two test pairs in which it is the earlier test give an average rate of gain of 0.688 points per year or more than twice the usual rate. And two test pairs in which when it is the later test give an average the rate of 0.027 points per years or practically nil. Table 3 in Appendix I shows that we can bring the WAIS-III in line with other tests by assuming that its norms inflate IQs by 2.34 points (over and above obsolescence). In 1997, when it was published, the results from that time to the present were of course unavailable. Therefore, it prompted speculation that the rate of IQ gains might have diminished (Flynn, 1998c); that speculation is now seen to be amiss.

It may be objected that all we have done is to show that the WAIS-III's norms are atypical. However, the alternative to considering that its norms are suspect is to doubt the norms of all four of the other tests that occur in comparison with it. It is logically possible that rather than the WAIS-III team selecting a substandard sample, the architects of all these other tests selected elite samples. If that is so, all tests but the WAIS-III are deflating IQs and many are being labeled as MR who should not qualify. But the odds are 15 to one against it.

This leaves the question of whether IQ gains and therefore obsolescence are much the same at low IQ levels as at other levels. This is crucial given that the criterion for mental retardation is 70 or below. Figure 5 shows that IQ gains are roughly constant at all levels on various versions of the WISC. This is reassuring in that it

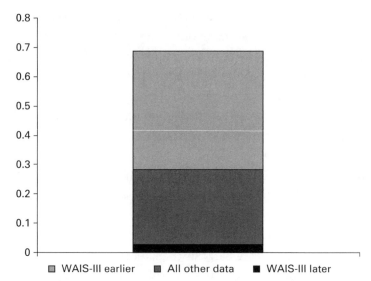

Figure 4 Note the inflated rate of gain when the WAIS-III is the earlier test and the virtually nil rate when the WAIS-III is the later test in a combination.

is the WISC, the Wechsler test for schoolchildren, that provides the IQs courts most value: those earned during the developmental period when a person is under 18.

When the WAIS, the Wechsler test for adults, is used to test defendants post-conviction, the pattern of gains is not so pretty. Naturally, the fact that the WAIS-III inflates IQs by 2.34 points (thanks to its substandard norms) distorts the pattern. Even when this is corrected, there is a problem with the WAIS-R due to a peculiar scoring convention. Subjects could get an IQ of 48 even though they got not a single item correct, which came to be called the tree-stump phenomenon in that an inert object would score at least 48 (no tree stump was actually tested). This distorts gains at very low IQ levels but the problem at 70, the crucial cutting line, is not too serious.

There are also minor distortions because in order to norm the WAIS you had to select a representative sample of American

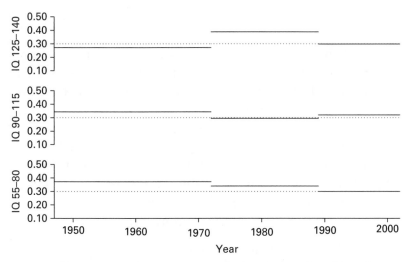

Figure 5 I use the WISC to test whether the IQ gains of American children have been relatively uniform (about 0.30 points per year) between 1947 and 2002, and whether that has been true at all IQ levels. The three IQ levels I have chosen are 125–140 (high), 90–115 (average), and 55–80 (low). At each level, the broken line represents a gain of exactly 0.30 points per year. The solid lines show how little actual rates of gain have deviated from that value (see Table 4 in Appendix I).

adults. With schoolchildren, as long as you locate a good sample of schools and test everyone, you are home free. Adults are not gathered together in one institution and can be located only if you visit all of their workplaces or homes. It is likely that adult samples can only be accurate to within a few points, particularly at low IQ levels. See Flynn (2006b) for a detailed discussion.

At last, we have all of the information needed to adjust scores: (1) For all Wechsler and Stanford–Binet IQ tests, deduct 0.30 points per year for every year that passed between the date when the test was normed and the date when the defendant took the test. (2) In addition, an extra 2.34 points should be deducted from WAIS-III scores on the grounds that that test gave inflated IQs even in the year in which it was normed (see Box 15).

Box 15

The only people who think it odd to adjust IQ scores for obsolescence are those who do not understand them. An IQ is not a thing like a loaf of bread. The scores are messages about how people rank compared to a representative sample of their age cohort. And when people are being scored against the wrong cohort (one from the past), we have to reinterpret scores by adjusting them. Thermometers send us messages about temperature. But in order to interpret them, we have to know whether the "norms" are Fahrenheit or Centigrade.

Compare the formulae for conversion:

(1) Temperature: $(C \times 9/5) + 32 = F$
(2) Intelligence: Test Score $- (I \times 0.3) = IQ$, where I is the interval between when the test was normed and when the subject sat; and the test is a Wechsler-Binet test administered in America. If the Wechsler test happens to be the WAIS-III, an extra 2.34 points should be deducted from the test score.

Certainly, the IQ formula is simpler than the temperature formula.

John Doe and his twin

Having derived a formula for adjusting IQs in capital cases, I wish to drive home the logic for its use. Therefore, I will review an actual case altered to avoid identification of the parties. To show how arbitrary unadjusted IQs can be, I will supply the defendant with an identical twin.

John Doe was convicted of murder and sentenced to death contingent on a determination of whether or not he was mentally retarded. He was born in 1967. During his developmental years, he was assessed only once: in 1975, at the age of 8, by Mary Smith a school psychologist. Fortunately, we have her report, which states that she gave him the WISC (normed 1947–1948) and not the WISC-R (normed 1972). This may seem odd given that the new (at that time) WISC-R was published in 1974. However, IQ tests are costly and schools tend to exhaust their old supply before purchasing the latest edition of a test.

Mary Smith was taught to assess adaptive functioning independently of IQ scores. In fact, school psychologists sometimes find it difficult to compartmentalize the two. You may find tell-tale signs in the report. In this case, Mary noted John's poor performance in reading and arithmetic despite extra tutoring, but then rejected a diagnosis of mental retardation on the basis of a WISC IQ score of 75. Today, we know something that she could not have known. Fully twenty-seven years had passed between the norming of the WISC and the day the defendant took it (1975 minus 1947–1948). Therefore, its norms were 8 IQ points out of date (27 × 0.3 points per year). So Johnny's score of 75 should have been lowered to 67, easily in the MR range.

Johnny's twin was more fortunate. He too was convicted of murder and sentenced to death contingent on a finding of whether or not he was MR. However, they were separated at birth and he was raised by aunt and went to a school in another district. When he was tested in 1975, at age 8, his school had trashed their copies of the old WISC because its budget allowed for purchasing the new WISC-R. On its newer norms, he scored 68. His school psychologist was no less under the spell of IQ scores than Mary Smith, but thanks to a score in the retardate range, she did not second guess the significance of his failure to profit from extra tutoring. Her report noted that she suspected that he was mentally retarded and might need special education.

Given the paucity of assessment during his developmental years, after conviction for murder, John Doe was interviewed by defense and prosecution psychologists. The defense psychologist noted a hesitancy and conceptual vagueness typical of the MR; the prosecution psychologist was surprised at the how alert and fluent he seemed. Therefore, despite the supposed importance of psychological assessment, IQ scores became decisive. The year was 1997, the year of the publication of the new WAIS-III. Since John was tested at the start of the year, the new test was not available and the old WAIS-R was used. The defense and prosecution psychologist both recorded IQs of 70. The defense was relieved to get an MR score but knew his case was weak. This marginal score was unlikely to prevail against the 75 that Johnny had received at school.

John's twin had a second piece of luck. He too was tested in 1997 but later in the year. Therefore, the new WAIS-III was used and he received a score of 67, an almost perfect match for the 68 he got at school. The defense was jubilant and the prosecution was in despair.

In sum, pure chance about what IQ test was taken when meant John Doe was at grave risk of execution and his twin at no risk at all. The only solution to this absurdity would be to adjust his IQ scores. We know that his 75 at school was inflated by twenty-seven years of obsolescence (1948 to 1975) and should have been 67. We know that his 70 on the WAIS-R was inflated by nineteen years of obsolescence (1978 to 1997) and should have been 64. We even know why his twin got 67 on the WAIS-III and not 64. His WAIS-III score was inflated by 2 or 3 points thanks to its substandard norms. But despite this, his luck held in that the WAIS-III at least did not boost him above the MR cutting line of 70.

Will our awareness of the lottery John Doe has lost help him to evade death? I am deeply pessimistic because of the nature of our adversarial system of justice. Prosecutors attempt to convict and get the maximum penalty. They hire psychologists who have a record of finding defendants mentally competent after interview. Most of those same experts will also make a case against using the formula I have recommended to adjust scores.

I have a document in front of me. There are no precedents in which psychologists making clinical assessments use my formula (the question should be judged on its merits). The twelve test combinations I used to measure IQ gains show wide variation around an average rate of gain of 0.30 points per year (that is inevitable, given sampling error, but where sampling is best, namely, the schoolchildren samples of the WISC, the variation is very small). It is possible that the WAIS-III is not at fault but rather the tests with which it is compared (but there are four of them and the odds against the WAIS-III are 15 to one). IQ gains have stopped in Scandinavia (what has that to do with American trends?).

The full reply I submitted to the court is reproduced in Appendix II. I have no hope that it or anything else will modify the behavior of prosecutors. The only hope is to send a message to the judges. You know why the experts for the defense and prosecution disagree and that this is inevitable. Give great weight to the IQ scores because, as rough as they are, they at least put a weight in the scales that is a matter of record. Understand why leaving them unadjusted is far worse than an approximate adjustment. Tawney (1931) once said that "letting an elephant loose in a crowd gives everyone but the beast and his rider an equal opportunity of being trampled." No judge can really believe that the Supreme Court intended to let an elephant loose on death row.

Bring the tires to me

The above argument makes a case against the equity of executing people thanks to obsolete norms. The case is based on the unfairness of a lottery and, therefore, does not need to address the question of whether subjects whose IQs are boosted by obsolete norms are really mentally retarded. But some of my passion stems from my conviction that this is often so. Thus far, the evidential basis of my conviction has been the Vineland Adaptive Behavior Scales: it showed that IQ gains over time were not accompanied by enhanced competence to cope with everyday life. However, the original source of my conviction lay elsewhere, namely, the capital cases that came my way. I read the case histories.

John Doe's case history shows that he never passed the test for a driver's license or held a job that required reasonable literacy or numeracy. Family and friends testified that he tended to lose focus if sent on errands. One boyhood companion testified that when the defendant and he were both 16 years of age, he pointed out a car and said: "That is Mrs. Smith's car. She and I are friends and she said I could borrow her tires. Would you go over and take them off and bring the tires to me."

Obsolete norms gave John Doe an IQ of 75 and if scored against norms set by his grandparents, he might have got a score as high as 86. So much the worse for obsolete norms. He was not mentally mature enough to be held responsible for his actions. Since that is what current norms show, they are to be preferred.

I cannot reveal identities, so the reader must remain ignorant of whether or not the public prosecutor secured John Doe's execution. I can assure you that his zeal was great. Whatever the outcome in this case, there are others in which obsolete norms, things so innocent in themselves, have played the role of executioner. The fate of these defendants, mainly black men, is an American tragedy, another item to be added to that long list that captures the black experience in America (Flynn & Dickens, under review).

7   What if the gains are over?

A wise man has the ability to reach sound conclusions about . . .
what conduces to the good life as a whole.
(Aristotle, *Ethics*, vi, 5, 1094b, 25–28)

There is no reason to believe IQ gains will go on forever. There may
remain few who have not absorbed the language of science to
whatever degree they can. The trend toward a higher ratio of adults
to children in the home may reverse. Any further drop in the birth
rate is likely to be outweighed by more solo-parent homes. There
must be some saturation point in our willingness to be challenged
by more conceptually demanding activities at work and at play.
Although IQ gains are still robust in America, they have stopped
in Scandinavia (Flynn & Weiss, in press; Schneider, 2006). Perhaps
Scandinavia is more advanced than America and its trends will
become universal, at least in developed nations.

The most obvious consequence of the end of IQ gains
would be that they would stop killing people on death row. If
there were no gains for thirty years or so, no one would have
IQs inflated by obsolete norms. Other consequences are less
obvious.

If IQ gains were to cease throughout the developed world
during the twenty-first century, this could give the developing
world a chance to catch up. Its people are overwhelmingly
still focused on the concrete and the distribution of scientific
spectacles has barely begun. There is good reason to predict that
developing nations in the twenty-first century will repeat what

---

Box 16

Over the last half century, America has seen the percentage of employed civilians who pursue professional, managerial, and technical occupations rise dramatically. The higher the percentage the less elite these groups become. Therefore, their mean IQ and the IQ threshold needed to gain entry to them fall over time (see Appendix I, Table 5 for detail).

Year	Percentage	Mean IQ	IQ threshold
1950	17.03	114.5	104
1960	18.86	114	103
1970	21.42	113	102
1980	25.25	112	100.5
1990	29.37	111.5	99
2000	33.48	110.5	98

---

happened in the developed world in the twentieth century: look at the huge gains reported from Kenya and Dominica (Daley *et al.*, 2003; Meisenberg *et al.*, 2005). Contrary to Lynn and Vanhanen (2002), I believe that IQ gaps between developed and developing nations are fluid and will diminish greatly in the twenty-first century. This prediction is subject to the proviso of no cataclysmic events, such as mass starvation or climate change, of the sort that renders all prediction impossible.

As for the future of nations like America and Britain, the prospect of the cessation of IQ gains poses an interesting question: could these nations go on meeting the demand for more and more managers and professionals and technicians? Over time, economic progress has meant the multiplication of managerial, professional, and technical jobs. As Box 16 shows, only 17 percent of Americans held such jobs in 1950 but by 2000, 33.5 percent did. There are IQ thresholds for various occupations, that is, minimum IQs such that if you fall below them, you are very unlikely to qualify as a doctor, scientist, nurse, technician, and so forth. The correlation between IQ and occupational status in the middle of this period was significant at about 0.65. The correlation generates estimates of the average IQ of those who fill jobs in the managerial, professional, and technical group and also of the IQ threshold. In 1980, a time when excellent data about the actual IQs of professionals were available, I found that such estimates were highly reliable (Flynn, 1991a, pp. 68–69 and 142–143).

An important fact: as elite occupations become less elite, that is, as the percentage of those who are managers, lawyers, and technicians rises, the IQ thresholds tend to fall. We can appreciate this intuitively by asking what would happen if literally everyone were a professional. Clearly, the IQ threshold would drop to zero. Box 16 shows that between 1950 and 2000, the average IQ for managers, professionals, and technicians dropped from 114.5 to 110.5. And the threshold dropped from 104 to 98.

Therefore, someone 2 points *below* the average IQ (set at 100) could meet the cognitive demands of elite jobs in the year 2000; while you had to be 4 points *above* the average IQ in 1950. That could be true only if the average person's cognitive skills had actually improved! America needed a real-world on-the-job performance gain equivalent to 6 IQ points, if it was to keep up with the demand for more and more elite jobs that the American economy created. The actual Wechsler IQ gain over those fifty years was about 16 points. This does not mean that the 10-point surplus was wasted: perhaps elite jobs are better performed today than they were fifty years ago.

On the other hand, if you assume that managerial, professional, and technical jobs are worse performed today, or that they have become less cognitively demanding, you can argue that none of America's IQ gains has affected elite job performance. Let those assumptions be tested by evidence. Until then, I will hypothesize that at least a significant portion of the IQ gains America enjoyed between 1950 and 2000 had real-world implications for the competent performance of elite work roles. Therefore, the cessation of IQ gains would be disturbing.

The SHAs and their enemies

There are more important things than economic progress. Even if developed nations do see the demise of IQ gains over time, this need not mean the end of cognitive progress. IQ gains are less than half the story of the cognitive history of the twentieth century. There are other intellectual qualities, namely, critical acumen and wisdom, that IQ tests were not designed to measure and do not measure and these are equally worthy of attention. Our obsession with IQ is one indication that rising wisdom has not characterized our time.

People may have assimilated some of the basic language of science and organize the world using its categories. They may be willing to take the hypothetical seriously. However, those achievements will be of limited value unless people take the next step. Have we begun to use science to enhance our ability to debate moral and social questions intelligently?

There is one encouraging development. Over the last century and a half, science and philosophy have invaded the language of educated people, particularly those with a university education, by giving them words and phrases that can greatly increase their critical acumen. Each of these terms stands for a cluster of inter-related ideas that virtually spell out a method of critical analysis applicable to social and moral issues. I will call them shorthand abstractions (or SHAs), it being understood that they are abstractions with peculiar analytic significance.

I will name ten SHAs followed by the date they entered educated usage (dates all from the *Oxford English Dictionary* on line), the discipline that invented them, and a case for their virtues. None of them appears in the verbal subtests of the various editions of the WISC or WAIS, that is, Similarities, Information, Comprehension, and Vocabulary. So if we want a test to measure the enhancement of critical acumen over time, we will have to invent one.

(1) **Market** (1776: economics). With Adam Smith, this term altered from the merely concrete (a place where you bought something) to an abstraction (the law of supply and demand). It provokes a deeper analysis of innumerable issues. If the government makes university education free, it will have to budget for more takers. If you pass a minimum wage, employers will replace unskilled workers with machines, which will favor the skilled. If you fix urban rentals below the market price, you will have a shortage of landlords providing rental properties. Just in case you think I have revealed my politics, I think the last a strong argument for state housing.

(2) **Percentage** (1860: mathematics). It seems incredible that this important SHA made its debut into educated usage less than 150 years ago. Its range is almost infinite. Recently in New Zealand, there was a debate over the introduction of a contraceptive drug that kills some women. It was pointed out that the extra fatalities from the drug amounted to 50 in one million (or 0.005 percent) while without it, an extra 1,000 women (or 0.100 percent) would have fatal abortions or die in childbirth.

(3) **Natural selection** (1864: biology). This SHA has revolutionized our understanding of the world and our place in it. It has taken the debate about the relative influences of nature and nurture on human behavior out of the realm of speculation and turned it into a science. Whether it can do anything but mischief if transplanted into the social sciences is debatable. It certainly did harm in the nineteenth century when it was used to develop foolish analogies between biology and society. Rockefeller was acclaimed as the highest form of human being that evolution had

produced, a use denounced even by William Graham Sumner, the great "Social Darwinist." I feel it has made me more aware that social groups superficially the same are really quite different because of their origins. Black unwed mothers who are forced into that status by the dearth of promising male partners are very different from unwed mothers who choose that status because they genuinely prefer it (Flynn & Dickens, under review).

(4) **Control group** (1875: social science). Recognition that before-and-after comparisons of how interventions affect people are usually flawed. We introduce an enrichment program in which preschool children go to a "play center" each day. It is designed to raise the IQ of children at risk of being diagnosed as mentally retarded. Throughout the program we test their IQs to monitor progress. The question arises, what has raised their IQs? The enrichment program, getting out of a dysfunctional home for six hours each day, the lunch they had at the play center, the continual exposure to IQ tests? Only a control group selected from the same population and subjected to everything but the enrichment program can suggest the answer.

(5) **Random sample** (1877: social science). Today, the educated public is much more likely to spot biased sampling than they were a few generations ago. In 1936, the Literary Digest telephone poll showed that Landon was going to beat Roosevelt for President and was widely believed, even though few had telephones except the more affluent. Nonetheless, lack of comprehension is frequent. Today I read a columnist I value for her intelligence in the *New Zealand Listener*. She told me that she did not believe that any poll of 1,000 people can be representative of the whole population.

(6) **Naturalistic fallacy** (1903: moral philosophy). That one should be wary of arguments from facts to values, for example, an argument that because something is a trend in evolution it provides a worthy goal for human endeavor.

(7) **Charisma effect** (1922: social science). Recognition that when a technique is applied by a charismatic innovator or disciples fired by zeal, it may be successful for precisely that reason. For example, a new method of teaching mathematics often works until it is used by the mass of teachers for whom it is merely a new thing to try.

(8) **Placebo** (1938: medicine). The recognition that merely being given something apparently endorsed by authority will often have a salutatory effect for obvious psychological reasons. Without this notion, a rational drugs policy would be overwhelmed by the desperate desire for a cure by those stricken with illness.

(9) **Falsifiable/tautology** (1959: philosophy of science). Tautologies (among other things) are definitions that appear to make a factual claim but actually remove a claim from the real world where it might be falsified. They are often used to evade testing what appears to be a historical claim against the evidence. Take the claim that the Scots, unlike the English, are a noble people. If you point to a Scot who is a liar and a cheat, you are likely to be told "Ah, he is na true Scot." The tautology, only good Scots count as Scots, is implicit. Take the claim that Christianity, on balance, has done more good than harm. If you point to the historical record of massacres and persecutions, you are likely to be told "But they were not real Christians." Apparently, only good Christians count as "real" Christians. The honor of any group can be defended by a definition of the group that excludes the wicked.

(10) **Tolerance school fallacy** (2000: moral philosophy). Somehow my coining this term has not made it into common currency, but no doubt that is merely a matter of time. It underlines the fallacy of concluding that we should respect the good of all because nothing can be shown to be good. This fallacy puts a spurious value on ethical skepticism by assuming that it entails tolerance, while the attempt to justify your ideals is labeled suspect as a supposed source of intolerance. It surfaced in William James, was embraced by anthropologists such as Ruth Benedict, and is now propagated by postmodernists who think they have invented it (Flynn, 2000a, ch. 9).

There is another set of concepts that superficially resemble SHAs but are actually wolves in SHAs' clothing. They may pretend to offer a method of analysis but the method is either mere words or bankrupt in some other way. Often, either by accident or design, they devour SHAs by denigrating them in favor of an ideology of anti-science. I will give a short list to illustrate the point but, sadly, it could be much longer.

(1) **Contrary to nature**. Although this is a special case of the naturalistic fallacy, it deserves mention because of its persistence. By calling something "unnatural," the speaker labels it intrinsically wrong in a way that is supposed to bar investigation of its consequences including beneficial ones. As Russell points out, the New England divines condemned lightning rods as unnatural because they interfere with the method God uses to punish the wicked (bolts of lightning). As Mill points out, nature has no purposes save those we read into it. It does not condemn gays, we do. When Haldane was asked what his study of nature had revealed to him about God's purposes, he replied "an inordinate fondness for beetles."

(2) **Intelligent design.** This implies a method in the sense
that one investigates nature to find signs of order imposed
by a rational agent. On one level it is not objectionable. It
is a respectable enterprise to update this ancient argument
for God's existence by appealing to the theories of modern
science (arguing that the conditions for the development
of the universe are too delicately balanced to be taken
simply as a given). But as an alternative to evolutionary
biology, it is entirely counterproductive. Rather than adding to our knowledge of nature, it delights in any present
failure of science to explain a phenomenon so it can insert
its monotonous refrain, "it was designed that way."

(3) **Race or gender science.** There is no implication that
those who speak of gender science share the viciousness
of those who spoke of "Jewish physics," but they are just as
muddled. In essence, there is only one method of understanding both the universe and human behavior, one
based on theory-formation, prediction, and attempts at
falsification by evidence. Not one of its critics has an alternative. The practice of science is flawed in all the ways in
which any human endeavor is flawed, that is, the interests
and prejudices of scientists color the problems they investigate, how they go about it, the theories they propose, and
the evidence they collect. The antidote is better science,
not endless and empty assertions that some epistemolog-
ical issue is at stake.

(4) **Reality is a text.** This phrase comes from Derrida but it
sums up the anti-science of our time. No one is willing to
plainly say what it means because its plain meaning is
ridiculous: that the world is a blank slate on which we
can impose whatever subjective interpretation we like
(Flynn, 1993a). The evidence against the assertion that all
theories are equally explanatory/non-explanatory was
refuted every time Derrida put on his spectacles. The

theory of optics explains why they worked and nothing else does so. As for the social sciences, how arbitrary is the choice between two theories of why most prostitutes in Boston were Anglicans (circa 1890)? The preachers who suspected that some subliminal text in their sermons was corrupting young women; or Sumner's observation that most prostitutes were graduates of orphanages and that the Anglican Church ran the orphanages.

This ersatz SHA is supposed to foster a method of investigation, but that method comes to no more than classifying the different kinds of texts we impose on the world. At its best, it merely copies the distinctions made by orthodox philosophy of science, which is careful to emphasize that some of these "texts" contain truths attested by evidence (physics) while others do not (aesthetic categories). Usually, it blurs these distinctions and asserts that they are all merely subjective, as if the text of an up-to-date timetable was not more valuable than the text of an out-of-date timetable *because* it tells the truth about something, namely, when busses actually depart. If all of this sounds absurd, that is not my fault.

The ersatz SHAs are evenly divided between the contributions of obscurantist churches and contemporary academics. The battle over the SHAs is being fought out within the walls of the universities. It is a contest pitting those who attempt to help students understand science, and how to use reason to debate moral and social issues, against those of whom it may be said that every student who comes within range of their voice is that little bit worse for the experience. There is no case for barring the latter from the university, but much depends on demonstrating the error of their ways.

Moral debate

Some of the SHAs, like the naturalistic fallacy, play an important role in moral debate. It is not alone. The concept of falsifiability plays an important role in debate that has moral relevance. My beginning students are often tempted by psychological egoism. The argument is that we act only on internalized needs or wants. If you seek money, it is because you want to. If you choose to lay down your life for another, you must want to. When the Christians died for their faith in the Roman arena, they would not have done so unless they wanted to, would they? So all human actions are basically selfish in motivation and the ethical merit of all is reduced to the common denominator of zero. Whatever action you propose to the psychological egoist is met by the same response. He would not have let himself be tortured to death to save his comrades unless he wanted to.

What seems the strength of this argument is actually its Achilles heel. Psychological egoism pretends to be a theory of human motivation. What would one have thought of Newton's theory of astronomy if it were compatible with any event in the heavens whatsoever? The job of a theory is to predict this rather than that, to predict that you will see Mercury here rather than there, not to say, well you might see it anywhere. A true theory may never actually be falsified, but we have no trouble imagining cases that would falsify it. So psychological egoism is bankrupt as a theory of motivation.

It is really a play on words with a hidden assumption. Unless I am under the spell of a hypnotist, I am autonomous in the sense that I choose to do whatever I do. Psychological egoism calls this choosing "responding to a want" but all that really means is that I act in terms of some value I internalize. What else? – Who can act on values that someone else internalizes? Some people internalize other-regarding principles and act on them, and we say that they have a moral motivation. Others internalize only self-regarding maxims and act on those, and we say that they are selfish and seek only what they want. Other-regarding actions often means sacrificing my wants in the sense that, with a heavy heart, I do my duty even though it causes me great suffering. You can call that doing what I want to do if you wish, but then we will simply distinguish wants sub-1 from wants sub-2: distinguish people who internalize only self-regarding "wants" from those who internalize other-regarding "wants." Most of us call the latter moral principles.

The psychological egoist can assert that other-regarding principles are peculiar in that, unlike other deeply internalized wants, they are impotent in actually causing human behavior. What exactly is his evidence for that? A wide range of human behavior seems explicable only on the assumption that people care more about the welfare of others than themselves. Something that is not a moral principle may underlie a moral principle of course. All of our internalized values may rest on a bed of brain physiology. So may all of our aesthetic judgments but, nonetheless, we judge some things to be beautiful and others ugly. After we have done our duty, we may take a certain satisfaction in the fact that we have lived up to our moral principles (if we are sill alive). That merely shows we love the good rather than do it out of a sheer intellectual perception that certain things are good. It hardly drains our actions of moral worth.

The twin of the concept of falsifiability is that of tautology. It is useful against a whole range of arguments that are obnoxious because they seek either to reserve a favored status to some alone on arbitrary grounds, or to grant immunity to some from an unfavorable status on arbitrary grounds.

Take the assertion, often made by human rights commissioners, that blacks or some other group subject to racism cannot themselves be accused of racism. If this translates into a tautology – blacks cannot be racists because my definition of racist stipulates that they must be non-black – it is a closed circle of words that makes no contact with reality. You may define roses as non-red. We cannot prevent you from speaking a private language if you want, but the practice is futile. Those of us who want language to describe the real world will humor you by using two labels: "rose" and "things that are like a rose in every way except that they are red." If a black lynches a Chinese boy for dating his daughter, he is racist in every way except that he is black – ho hum.

Similar arguments are used to arbitrarily exclude a group from a favored status. Some feminists deny that men can be feminists. At my university some years ago, there was a male student whose dedication to the cause of women's rights was extraordinary. The radical feminist group was quite unwilling to call him a feminist but he drove them crazy. If qualifying meant that you had to picket beauty contests, he was on the picket line. If you had to bite a policeman on the ankle, he would bite a policeman on the ankle.

Now it is perfectly sensible to assert that you have never met a man whose behavior showed that he truly held feminist principles. But whatever criterion you set, both men and women must qualify if they meet it, unless you want to commit the absurdity of saying only female feminists are feminists. This is on a par with a definition of socialist that stipulates that only gay socialists are socialists. You may predict that men are unlikely to hold feminist principles deeply enough unless they experience what women experience, for example, being raped. But most women have never been raped, so this translates into no man can imagine the horror of rape. That can be falsified. Whenever I see films about homosexual rape in prisons, my horror is lively indeed.

Although various SHAs deserve credit for clarifying moral debate, the sheer fact that logic and the hypothetical have become detached from the concrete makes a powerful contribution. Indeed, without a free-wheeling use of logic and the hypothetical, much moral debate would never get off the ground. The most primitive kind of racist is a color racist who says that simply being black excludes you from a favored status, that is, exemption from slavery, eligibility to vote, marrying who you please, and so forth. Let us see how we can use logic and the hypothetical to drive him out of one shelter after another.

Box 17

When I was a young lecturer and chair of a group dedicated to equal rights, a university official harassed me and eventually discharged me because of my politics. I do not think he was a racist but simply had political ambitions and thought our group might do something to taint him. One of his black servants was friendly to our group and it was a temptation to get her to put a pill in his food that would slowly blacken his skin. The image of his peering into the mirror each morning was attractive. Sadly, following the example of Martin Luther King, our group's ethical code forbad it.

If racists say that people ought to barred from certain desirable things simply because they are black, we can follow R. M. Hare (1963) and ask what they would say if their own skin turned black, perhaps because we sneaked a pill in their food or because of some pollutant in the water supply (see Box 17). When Hare imagined someone answering this question in the affirmative, he made the mistake of calling him a "fanatic," which provoked the response that you could just as easily call someone willing to suffer for their ideals a hero.

What we ought to say to such a racist is that he is not suffering for his ideals but for a principle in which he does not really believe. He is willing to lay down his life for an absurdity, namely, that color nullifies personal traits as criteria for assessing human beings. No historical racist has ever said that. Hitler did not tell the Germans that they were superior simply because they were white or were Aryans; rather he told them that they were more creative, courageous, and commanding than the rest of us. Imagine a Nazi orator telling his German audience that they deserved to be ruled by Africans just because the two groups had exchanged skin colors.

Imagine a book reviewer. He tells his readers to avoid one book because it has a black cover and to buy another because it has a white cover. The next day he tells them to do the reverse because new editions have reversed the colors. Even racists would give up reading this book reviewer in favor of one who deigned to discuss plot, character, dialogue, and style. If racists grant that it is absurd to ignore the traits of fictional characters when nothing is at stake but a good read, can they seriously contend that we should ignore the traits of real people when the stakes are who has a right to a decent life?

That is why real-world racists always eschew pure color racism in favor of asserting a correlation between color and despised personal traits. Blacks are said to be stupid, permanently immature, and congenitally prone to rape. Once logic has forced racists to enter the real world and assert factual hypotheses, falsification by evidence follows automatically. We can point to thousands of counterexamples, the thousands of blacks of genius or talent ranging from Saint Augustine and Victor Hugo to Paul Robeson and Thomas Sowell. The last word belongs to Frederick Law Olmsted (1969). When traveling through the ante-bellum American South, he heard laws against educating blacks defended on the grounds that blacks could no more learn to read or write than animals or maniacs. He asked why, then, there were no laws on the books forbidding people to teach animals and maniacs.

It is not just racists who can be punished by the tool of logic. Many today are strong advocates of animal rights. I supervised a student who believed it was immoral to spray mosquito larvae. It was the thin edge of the wedge: the next step was medical experiments on cats and dogs. I asked the obvious question: if it was wrong to kill fetal mosquitoes even though the consequence would be the death of many innocent people, what of killing a fetal human being to preserve the quality of life of one person? She resolved the dilemma by marrying the proprietor of a Persian restaurant who persuaded her that eating lamb was not wrong. He did not quite persuade her to put her own pet lamb on the menu.

Logical consistency in the abortion debate would force many to reconsider their position. What if an infant was born in a permanent coma and you were the only person alive who could bring her out of it? You would have to experience a series of blood transfusions for nine months and, toward the end, undergo a physical debilitation that would curtail your normal activities. You would be committed to a painful bone graft if the case so required and there would be a small risk of losing your life. Once all this was done, there might be another child that required the same treatment. Logic can also prevent us from being too glib. Some say that they approve of abortion only before the month at which the fetus could survive separate from the mother. But science with the invention of an artificial womb might push that back to zero. You should really believe what you say in moral debate and not pay lip service to distinctions simply because they are convenient. You may find yourself trapped by logic and committed to forbidding abortion flatly.

Finally, it is fashionable to forbid moral criticism across cultural lines. But logic forbids this from being used arbitrarily. In New Zealand, there are those who refuse to criticize Maori (the indigenous Polynesian population) for sexism, such as the practice of forbidding women to speak at important meetings. If they really believe that it is wrong to deliver a moral indictment across cultural lines, Maori should be told that they cannot accuse Europeans of injustice. The rule against cross-cultural value judgments has some commonsense validity, but often it is used to construct a one-way street.

This will have to serve as an illustration of the role that the SHAs and liberated logic can play in moral debate. Those who have acquired a taste for the subject will find more in my last book, *How to defend humane ideals* (Flynn, 2000a) – see Box 18.

Box 18

This book (*How to defend humane ideals*) tries to banish the moral confusion that plagues our time, that is, it clarifies the consequences of ethical skepticism. Most thinking people today feel trapped between belief in outmoded truth tests in ethics, the will of God, the intentions of nature, and so forth on the one hand, and a sense of desperation that even their most cherished ideals are "merely subjective" on the other. I accept that we have to internalize humane-egalitarian ideals, that is, no one will feel an obligation to be humane except those who have the appropriate commitment. However, I try to show how those of us who do have such a commitment are superior to our opponents in that we need not take refuge in illogic or sweep any of what science tells us under the carpet. As the reader knows, I also refute the "tolerance school fallacy," the contention that there is some virtue in regarding all moral ideals as equal because that entails tolerance.

Practical wisdom

Higher critical awareness in both social analysis and moral debate would be a very good thing indeed. However, the highest level of cognitive progress is enhanced wisdom. Wisdom is knowledge of how to live a good life and, if one is fortunate enough to understand other peoples and their histories as well, it is knowledge of how to make a better world. Someone can have great critical acumen and lack wisdom. The former is an intellectual virtue, while the latter exists only when human beings integrate the intellectual and moral virtues into a functional whole. Wisdom focuses perfected intellect and perfected character on the same object. As Plato shows so wonderfully in the image of the chariot, one cannot know the good without loving the good. It would be like saying one knew what made a great painting beautiful without having any appreciation of its beauty.

Box 19

My candidates for the greatest minds of Western civilization would be Archimedes, Pythagoras, Plato, Aristotle, Newton, Gauss, and Einstein. Four of the seven are ancient Greeks. Plato may have been even more intelligent than Aristotle but the latter is closer to the truth, which gives hope to those of us who are far less bright. You would enjoy reading Plato because of his wonderful style (Flynn, 2000a, ch. 2). All we have left of Aristotle is a massive collection of what may have been a student's lecture notes and these are difficult. The notion of one's ideas surviving only through a student's lecture notes makes every academic feel despair.

Aristotle argued that you cannot claim knowledge of the art of good living unless you practice the art. I may know what a good backhand in tennis looks like, but if I cannot hit one, I cannot savor the body's wonderful coordination when it is done and do not experience the life of meticulous practice that is a functional part of the performance (see Box 19).

Aristotle spells out the traits of people of practical wisdom. They must value others rather than just themselves or they cannot fully participate in the kind of human society that makes good living possible. In Book III of the *Politics*, he tells us that society is not merely a market because we can do business with foreigners; it is not a mutual security pact because we can have military alliances with foreigners; it is not intermarriage because one can marry a foreigner; it is not occupying the same territory because the occupants of the same city can treat one another as if they were enemies; it is not even doing no harm to one another because one can be kind to foreigners. There must be a cherished way of life woven out of friendships, civic cooperation, and social pursuits, but even this is not enough unless it is crowned by mutual moral concern among fellow citizens. All must count as worthy of justice: none must be denied full and proper participation in the cherished way of life (Aristotle, *Politics*, iii, 9, 1280a, 26–40 and 1280b, 1–40).

Certain loves makes the good life impossible. The Spartans' love of power or victory in war turned the concept of the good person into the caricature of the good soldier. The love of money confuses the good person with the successful oligarch and corrupted the Carthaginians even though they sought to level differences of wealth by exporting their poor to other cities (Aristotle, *Politics*, ii, 9, 1271b, 1–9; *Politics*, ii, 11, 1273a, 21–40 and 1273b, 1–24).

However, love of the good is not enough. The person of practical wisdom must also have certain moral and intellectual virtues: self-discipline and temperance so they can resist temptations to deviate from the good life; courage so their judgment will not be blinded by fear; prudence or the knowledge of means to ends; understanding of the fact that every parent or teacher creates a social dynamic peculiar to themselves and that no one method will serve all. And above all, sympathetic empathy or the ability to look at the world through the eyes of others and resonate with how they feel (Aristotle, *Ethics*, iii, 6–12 and vi, 5–11).

Towards WICA theory

The aim of WICA theory would be to measure wisdom, intelligence, and critical acumen on the levels of social trends and individual differences. The central question is whether we can devise tests for these traits or whether we will have to be satisfied with informal measures. The issue is already decided for intelligence although, as we have seen, even there informal measures do something that the tests cannot. We had to turn to things like TV programming and leisure activities that had become more cognitively demanding to show that rising IQ scores had an impact on the real world.

Measures of critical acumen

As for an informal measure, Rosenau and Fagan (1997) compare the 1918 debate on women's suffrage with recent debates on women's rights and make an excellent case that the latter show less contempt for logic and relevance. Note the setting, namely, debate that goes into the Congressional Record. That congressmen have become less willing to give their colleagues a mindless harangue to read does not necessarily mean that presidential speeches to a mass audience have improved. This study stands alone but there is no reason why we should not develop a significant literature. A survey covering fifty years of news stories and opinion essays in semi-serious publications like *Newsweek* and *Time* would be informative, and might reveal enhanced sophistication of analysis and a growing tendency to supplement rhetoric with reason.

As a first attempt at a formal measure of critical acumen, I have designed the SOCRATES (**So**cial **Cr**iticism and **A**nalysis **Tes**t). It consists of fourteen items, one for each SHA and ersatz SHA. The trick is to test for awareness of the SHA without actually naming it. It is designed for final-year students at university and should take about seventy minutes, time for a five-minute paragraph on each item, but subjects can take up to ten minutes if they wish.

(1) Everything can be turned into a commodity for profit (market).
(2) Highway driving is safer than city driving because the latter causes more accidents (percentage).
(3) If someone says that black doctors are worse than white doctors, or even that they are better than white doctors, they are talking nonsense (differential selection).
(4) Children in solo-parent homes have lower IQs than children in two-parent homes; therefore, if we can eliminate solo-parent homes, we will raise the mean IQ (need to control for confounding variables).

(5) I would have more faith in public opinion polls if their samples included 10,000 voters (random sample).

(6) The age at which a fetus can survive outside the womb decides the question of what limits should be put on abortion (naturalistic fallacy).

(7) Two teachers invent new but very different ways of teaching arithmetic; one gets far better results than the other and claims that her method is superior (charisma effect).

(8) The definition of a cure is anything that cures sick people (placebo).

(9) No real Christian lacks charity (falsifiability).

(10) Never be judgmental (tolerance school fallacy).

(11) Margarine has artificial additives (contrary to nature).

(12) Watch makers make watches work (intelligent design).

(13) All peoples have their own sciences; our kind of science just works somewhat better than most (notion of alternatives to the scientific method).

(14) I live in my world and you live in yours (reality is a text).

Needless to say, the criterion of a correct answer is not whether the candidate agrees but what distinctions they make in answering. Competent watch makers do make watches that work, but the watches work because of the mechanical principles that govern them. We all live in our own cognitive and emotional worlds but we share a common physical universe (special allowance is made here for philosophy majors who start talking about Berkeley's idealism). If our university graduates, regardless of specialization, cannot say something sensible about such items, we may be training for vocations but we are hardly educating. I make no apology because someone with a high IQ may do badly on this test because they have been systematically mis-educated.

My suggestion that this test be administered to final-year university students assumes that the prerequisites for coping are sixteen years of schooling and an IQ of about 110. But it would be interesting to see what the IQ thresholds really are as scores rise from 0 to 14 sensible answers.

Measures of wisdom

The informal measures of wisdom are social statistics critically evaluated and the quality of decision-making. I am skeptical that the level of wisdom rose in the twentieth century, but my case grows stronger as one goes from personal to political to international behavior.

On the personal level, the interrelated virtues of temperance and self-discipline have had to cope with new challenges. Avner Offer (2006) provides a brilliant analysis of how technological progress and affluence have contributed to the obesity epidemic. Before pre-prepared foods existed, meals required effort to cook. Before even middle-class children had much money, food intake was restricted to mealtimes at which adults were present. I never knew a child who left home with money in his or her pocket except to go on an errand or to an occasional film. The notion that I was an independent consumer never occurred to me. Both rich and poor children now spend much time in shopping malls. I would have thought this as bizarre as spending a day in a butcher's shop watching someone chop meat.

Obesity is less common among upper- than lower-income earners. It is easier for the former to exercise virtue. Even if the mother works, fathers often help. Together they are more likely to overcome fatigue and show the self-discipline necessary to plan and prepare a healthy diet. They are more likely to curb their own appetites and thereby set a better example. They are more likely to supervise what their children eat at school and try to forbid what has immediate appeal. But there are plenty of cases in which affluence and obesity go together. Even if only upper-income earners are considered, we are still struggling to develop new social restraints to do the job of the old. Preachers used to give sermons castigating gluttony and sloth and one had to confess them as sins. No one would give such a sermon today.

Current political behavior shows an unwillingness to accept the restrictions on growth necessary to preserve our habitat. This too is a new challenge and we may have to transcend the wisdom of previous times. The central question is whether or not we have developed an appetite for the endless acquisition of goods that, particularly as it sweeps through China and India, makes self-restraint impossible. That question turns on the evidence for two propositions.

First, whether more and more goods bring more and more happiness. If they do, we are in trouble because it is hard to ask people to settle for less happiness. Here the news is good. Setting aside the poor, reported happiness (are you "very happy," "pretty happy," or "not too happy") did not increase in America over twenty years of growing affluence. Reported happiness in Japan did not increase between 1958 and 1987 despite a five-fold per capita income increase. There is no evidence that the members of very affluent societies are happier than those of somewhat less affluent societies (Blanchflower, Oswald, & Warr, 1993; Easterlin, 1995; Oswald, 1997, p. 1819; Veenhoven, 1993).

Second, do we value having more goods than others, which is to say have we gone from seeking possessions to seeking economic status? If so, an open-ended pursuit of more and more possessions will be difficult to avoid. Everyone cannot have more than the average person and even those above average will know a neighbor who has more. In terms of logic, it is possible to tell people there will still be a hierarchy of wealth even if the average wealth is less, and that they will have just as much chance of attaining a privileged place on it as they do now. But in terms of psychology, the command "no more" appears to freeze your present position on the hierarchy rather than allow you to aspire to a higher place.

Here the news is bad. Some of the evidence is anecdotal. The emergence of a huge Russian industry that manufactures the appearance of affluence: you can impress others with forged documents proving that you were on an expensive holiday even though you took a modest one. The premium paid for designer labels on goods no better than other goods so that one can flaunt one's affluence. The really disturbing evidence comes from the happiness literature. I refer to the evidence that possessions affect reported happiness in relative terms (I have a better house than most other Americans) rather than in absolute terms (Easterlin, 1974; Frey & Stutzer, 1999). Competition for possessions without a rationally imposed limit engenders pessimism about acceptance of the restraints necessary to avoid ecological disaster.

Competition for possessions also creates a downward spiral destructive of civic virtue. Those who wish to maximize their economic status are reluctant to pay taxes and this diminishes state provision of health, education, and security against misfortune. As the quality of state provision declines, it becomes imperative to maximize private wealth for reasons of security even if status seeking is set aside. Even principled socialists will pay fees to jump the queue for medical care and to get education for their children in schools that are not a test of physical survival. The more that is true, the more you resent any dollar leaving your pocket in tax, so public provision drops further, so willingness to be taxed drops further, and so forth. Indeed, since only a few can amass the fortune needed to provide self-security, no amount of money you can realistically hope to acquire is enough.

The existence of atomized actors forced to provide for their own security is always destructive of concern for others. The quest for absolute security by America and Russia during the arms race allocated resources away from too many goods to enumerate. I do not believe people really want lack of temperance to destroy the quality of life or the humanity of the body politic. On one level, everyone prefers Aristotle's polity to a mutual security pact. But wisdom requires that we love the good and love it enough to temper our desires.

On the international level, there is little evidence in favor of enhanced wisdom. Love of war is no longer respectable but the inordinate love of country that goes beyond patriotism to nationalism still cheats us of empathy. America today is no more aware of how to use its preponderant power without alarming other nations than the Kaiser was a century ago (Flynn, in press). Blair is far less aware of how little he influences American policy than Churchill was at Yalta. Enoch Powell and Michael Foot once agreed that no army can do the job of a police force without being de-humanized, at least not in a foreign country whose sociology it does not comprehend. America discovered this in Vietnam and yet cannot remember it today and is surprised to find its troops reacting with atrocities to the frustrations they encounter. Statesmen are no more aware of the limitations of force. They think they can impose political unity where there is no social unity.

Some of today's statesmen have a wider vision, of course. George Bush senior was superior to George Bush junior and Rabin was superior to Sharon. But some good statesmen have always existed: witness Congressman Reed versus President McKinley over the Spanish-American War. If seeking counsel from a higher power is evidence of wisdom, there is continuity from McKinley to the present. In his diary, McKinley tells us that when troubled about the war's aftermath, he knelt down in prayer and in the still hours of the morning heard a voice telling him to annex the Philippines.

The subjectivity of such a balance sheet kindles a desire for a formal measure of practical wisdom. Nevo and Flynn developed the HED-VQ (Humane Egalitarian Democratic Values Questionnaire). This is a self-report questionnaire composed of 46 items culled from *How to defend humane ideals* (Flynn, 2000a), lexical definitions of democracy, equality, and human rights, and various UN documents (especially the Universal Declaration of Human Rights of 1948). The same items are presented in both Part A, where candidates register their own strength of agreement with the ideal, and Part B, where candidates register their impression of how much their own society fulfills the ideal.

A pilot version of the HED-VQ was administered to a sample of 100 undergraduate students at the University of Haifa (Nevo, 2002). There was a considerable gap between what the students endorsed as ideal and what they observed around them. Five items stood out as almost universally endorsed (4.45 to 4.75 on a five-point scale) but often absent from Israeli society (2.60 to 2.67): everyone who is willing and capable of working should get a job; everyone should have equal access to job opportunities; no one should be discriminated against because of their race; no one should be discriminated against because of their religion; a reasonable environment should be preserved for future generations even if this means economic sacrifices now. Women had higher ideals than men (4.45 to 4.19) and were slightly more critical of their society (3.11 to 3.27). The rank order of ideals endorsed was much the same for both sexes.

If measures of commitment to humane ideals are combined with measures of character and empathy, a formal test of wisdom might result. Let us hope that scholars will build on the pioneering work of Duckworth and Seligman (2005) and develop more formal measures of self-control (they were the ones who used questionnaires and children receiving two dollars so long as they could resist spending one dollar). Let us hope that all the work being done on measuring EQ leads to a good measure of empathy. After all, people are doing excellent work in testing whether apes can see the world though the eyes of their fellows, so the task of measuring the same trait in humans should not be insuperable.

It may be said that my criterion of wisdom has a humane-egalitarian bias. Nietzsche had high intelligence and critical acumen: should he not be credited with an anti-humane brand of wisdom? Flynn (2000a) attempts to show that Nietzsche could not defend his ideals in the light of logic and social science. Here it is enough to say that without humane-egalitarian ideals society withers away and that without them our prospects for a civilized future are bleak.

Sic itur ad astra

The ultimate goal of WICA theory would be to understand the role of intelligence in acquiring critical acumen and the role of both in acquiring wisdom. This modest objective may lie some distance in the future. In any event, it would be good to develop new instruments. Thus far, the cognitive skills enhanced have been caught in the net of current IQ tests. It will be sad if more important cognitive skills begin to escalate and go unnoticed because they are unmeasured.

We must hope that the industrial revolution, the factory that made IQ gains inevitable, has not manufactured appetites that wisdom cannot tame. Affluence has decadence as a historical companion and decadence turns progress into retrogression, both intellectual and moral. However, elderly men are prone to pessimism. Those more attuned to the present may see the future more clearly.

8   Knowing our ancestors

> It is a wise child that knows its own father.
> (Homer, *The Odyssey*, I, 215–216)

> Everything is what it is, and not another thing.
> (Bishop Joseph Butler)

Even those who believe I have provided a coherent interpretation of massive IQ gains over time may wish for something better. The fact that the differences between our minds and those of our ancestors are subtle only makes the task of reading them more difficult. If only we could get into a time machine and go back and study our ancestors directly.

Colom, Flores-Mendoza, and Abad (in press) may have given us the next best thing. They did a study of children aged 7 to 11 years in Brazil. They compared an urban sample from the city of Belo Horizonte (tested in 1930 on the Draw-a-Man test) with both an urban sample from that city (tested in 2002) and a rural sample (tested in 2004). Over seventy-two years, urban children had gained 17 IQ points, but the contemporary urban–rural gap was even larger at 31.5 points. Present-day urban children and rural children were also compared on Raven's Colored Matrices and the WISC Arithmetic and Digit Span subtests. The urban–rural gap was 31 IQ points on Raven's and 15 points on the WISC. The rural children came from Americaninha, a district without hospitals, banks, postal service, and TV (only 8 percent of homes have electricity).

So here we have a group of people who have much the same IQ profile as our ancestors and whose social conditions are similar. The people of Belo Horizonte and Americaninha should be studied in depth, which suggests a final research design, albeit one specific to those locales.

Design VI There are five hypotheses:

(1) When the full WISC-IV is administered, urban–rural subtest score differences will not match subtest g loadings.
(2) Score differences on Similarities will approach Raven's differences.
(3) Interviews with Americaninha subjects will reveal that the use of logic and the hypothetical is tied to concrete applications.
(4) Piagetian tests will show a large urban–rural difference on whether people have achieved the formal operational level or merely the concrete level.
(5) Kinship studies of the urban and rural subjects will show environment too feeble to account for the massive urban–rural IQ difference.

Everything we have assumed about IQ gains can actually be tested.

I would like to make a final plea to those who emphasize test sophistication. Contemplate the environment of the children of Americaninha: does it seem reasonable that the cognitive disadvantages this environment inflicts are limited to test sophistication? I join in the appeal Cromwell addressed to the Long Parliament: "I beseech you, in the bowels of Christ, to consider whether or not you may be mistaken." Cromwell did not, of course, put the same question to himself.

Sadly, it is time to make an end. I cannot say I enjoyed the task of trying to make sense of massive IQ gains over time. However, they did show how little we really knew about intelligence and knowledge of ignorance is progress. They also produced some pleasurable correspondence (see Box 20).

> **Box 20**
>
> A professor of sexology told me that however stupid human beings were in the past, they could still procreate because even animals can do that. I had to agree. Someone who herds reindeer in Finland asked if medieval people had IQs below zero. I replied that such a thing made no sense, but it was quite possible to have negative critical acumen, witness the rise of postmodernism. The Potato Institute in Poland told me they found my work of interest. I did not dare ask why.

I have tried to break a steel chain of ideas that circumscribed our ability to see what was happening all around us and to appreciate what was possible. Until recently, the notion of a unitary intelligence subject to the glacial pace of brain evolution held sway, with the corollary that dysgenic reproduction was slowly eroding cognitive potential.

We now see that society can so enhance the power of the human mind that we probably have much time to reverse a dysgenic trend before it has important consequences. We also know that society can make differential progress without facing some kind of psychometric veto. It is good that 100-meter speed can improve without waiting for the high jump to tag along. It is good that we can improve our innovative thinking skills without waiting for the schools to upgrade arithmetical reasoning. Unless that were so, we might wait forever. It is good that society's priorities and the social multipliers it uses to get its way are contemptuous of factor analysis.

What follows is my version of the cognitive history of the twentieth century. I see it as a great romance. Science altered our lives and then liberated our minds from the concrete. This history has not been written because, as children of our time, we do not perceive the gulf that separates us from our distant ancestors: the difference between their world and the world seen through scientific spectacles. Moreover, because our ability to cope with the concrete demands of everyday life has not been much enhanced, our distant ancestors appear fully human. People use their minds to adapt to the demands of their social environment. Long before the beginning of the twentieth century, people felt a strong need to be cognitively self-sufficient in everyday life; and long before 1900, virtually everyone who could meet the demands of everyday life had done so. The small percentage that cannot has not varied much over the last 100 years.

Before 1900, most Americans had a few years of school and then worked long hours in factories, shops, or agriculture. Their world was largely concrete. The only artificial images they saw were drawings or photographs both of which tended to be representational. Aside from basic arithmetic, non-verbal symbols were restricted to musical notation (for an elite) and playing cards (except for the religious). People's minds were focused on ownership, the useful, the beneficial, and the harmful. Kinship and church provided identity. Slowly society began to demand that the mass of people come to terms with the cognitive demands of secondary education, and contrary to the confident predictions of the privileged, they met that challenge to a large degree. Mass graduation from secondary school had profound real-world effects. The search for identity became a more individual quest. Education created a mass clientele for books, plays, and the arts, and culture was enriched by contributions from those whose talents had hitherto gone undeveloped.

After 1950, the emergence of a new visual culture and perhaps a resistance to the ever-enhanced demands of classroom subjects brought progress to an end in areas like school mathematics and interpretation of serious literature. Nonetheless, post-1950 IQ cognitive gains have been significant. More and more people began to put on scientific spectacles. As use of logic and the hypothetical moved beyond the concrete, people developed new habits of mind. They became practiced at solving problems with abstract or visual content and more innovative at administrative tasks.

The scientific ethos provided the prerequisites for this advance. However, once minds were prepared to attack these new problems, certain social triggers and multipliers enhanced performance greatly. Post-1950 affluence meant that people sought cognitive stimulation from leisure. It meant parents had to rear fewer children and they became preoccupied with affording their children a cognitively stimulating environment. Schools became filled with children and teachers less friendly to rote learning, and the world of work offered more and more professional and managerial jobs. These jobs both required and stimulated the new habits of mind.

The expanded population of secondary-school graduates was a prerequisite for the chief educational advance of the post-1950 era, that is, the huge increase in the number of university graduates. These graduates have gone the farthest toward viewing the world through scientific spectacles. They are more likely to be innovative and independent, and can therefore meet professional and managerial demands. A greater pool of those suited by temperament and therefore inclination to be mathematicians or theoretical scientists or even philosophers, more contact with people who enjoy playing with ideas for its own sake, the enhancement of leisure, these things are not to be despised. And all of this has come about without an upgrading of the human brain through better genes or environmental factors that have a direct impact on brain physiology.

Whether the twentieth century saw an enhancement of critical acumen should be investigated. There is some evidence that members of Congress are less obtuse today at least in speeches designed for their peers. At a minimum, I would anticipate a general trend toward elementary market analysis of economic proposals and higher standards of evidence, particularly in regard to medical claims and claims about the state of public opinion.

Someone should do a systematic analysis of editorials and opinion essays in leading newspapers and periodicals aimed at a mass but educated readership. As for wisdom, that is almost undoubtedly going to be a subjective assessment. We should design formal measures of these traits so that historians at the end of the twenty-first century have a quantified record of trends.

There are signs that IQ gains may cease in developed nations in the twenty-first century but may take off in the developing world. This would eliminate the IQ gap that separates those two worlds and refute those who see the lower IQs of developing nations as a largely fixed cause of lack of economic progress. It would show that industrialization and IQ rise in tandem and boost one another in a cycle of reciprocal causation. All of this assumes that problems of food supply, water supply, energy supply, and climate do starve the poor and debase the rich.

Despite static IQ, the developed world may enjoy a century of cognitive progress just as exciting as the last 100 years. Science has given us wonderful concepts we can use to train our critical faculties. But the opponents of science are well organized. Their tactics are sound because they realize the crucial role of education. If they can fill the schools with nonsense, they win. Although they do not recognize them as such, they have powerful allies within the universities in academics who teach appealing brands of learned nonsense. The universities of the twenty-first century will be the battleground of armies for and against the SHAs. If the universities remember what they are supposed to be all about, they can create the vanguard of what would be nothing less than a new cognitive species, self-aware and beyond blind convention to a degree that only a few of their predecessors could hope to attain. Nietzsche hoped for the emergence of a few "over-men" who would be autonomous and brutal. We can hope to educate millions of people who will be autonomous and humane.

Now at last, we can "answer" the solemn question of whether massive IQ gains should be called intelligence gains. Let me put a proposition: if a genetic mutation had preceded this cognitive advance, one that affected the size or configuration or neural density of the human brain, everyone would use the label "intelligence." We would say that our physiological limitations had chained logic and the hypothetical to the concrete, and thank God for the genes that had liberated us. But since our minds have always had the needed brain capacity and environment has been the instrument of advance, I suspect that most will feel constrained to talk about "better education." Words have no magical power. Massive IQ gains are what they are and do not become another thing thanks to a particular label. The best shorthand description I can offer is this. During the twentieth century, people invested their intelligence in the solution of new cognitive problems. Formal education played a proximate causal role but a full appreciation of causes involves grasping the total impact of the industrial revolution.

I hope that this book finds readers more comfortable with the concept of intelligence at its end than they were at its beginning. I have attempted to do twelve things:

(1) Define the primitive concept of intelligence and list its components.

(2) Show how IQ tests like the WISC make a stab at measuring its components or, at least, at measuring the form intelligence takes in modern industrial nations; and indicate how traditional tests may need to be supplemented.

(3) Describe what makes the components of intelligence cohere (individual differences in general intelligence) and explode (the social multiplier) and fly apart (the infinite variety of socials trends).

(4) Clarify the roles of genes and environment.

(5) Suggest a bit of what we know and do not know about brain physiology.

(6) Offer a program for research and some research strategies.

(7) Describe both the importance and limitations of intelligence.

(8) Clarify the sense in which intelligence increased and did not increase in the twentieth century.

(9) Show that ignorance about IQ gains can be a matter of life and death.

(10) Isolate some of the wonderful concepts our scientific spectacles have given us.

(11) Describe how we could build a temple of reason on that foundation.

(12) Do some cognitive archeology, that is, go back to enter the world of our ancestors.

Surely, I cannot have failed in all twelve of these tasks.

When I was a child, I was sometimes allowed, as a special treat, to look at my grandmother's stereopticon slides. You looked at two pictures side by side through a pair of glasses and they blended into one three-dimensional image of a peculiar world, often long-skirted women wearing floral hats and holding bicycles. Today, I realize that riding a bicycle was the mark of a confident and modern woman liberated from the strictures of Victorian society. And now, through the lens of my grandmother's mind, I think I can see a picture of that distant pre-scientific world.

Appendix I: Tables

Table 1 WISC subtest and Full Scale IQ gains: 1947 to 2002

	WISC to WISC-R 1947.5–72 Gain 24.5 yrs (SD = 3)	WISC-R to WISC-III 1972–89 Gain 17 yrs (SD = 3)	WISC-III to WISC-IV 1989–2001.75 Gain 12.75 yrs (SD = 3)	WISC to WISC-IV 1947.5–2001.75 Gain 54.25 yrs (SD = 3)	WISC to WISC-IV 1947.5–2001.75 IQ Gain 54.25 yrs (SD = 15)
Information	0.43	−0.3	0.3	0.43	2.15
Arithmetic	0.36	0.3	−0.2	0.46	2.30
Vocabulary	0.38	0.4	0.1	0.88	4.40
Comprehension	1.20	0.6	0.4	2.20	11.00
Picture Completion	0.74	0.9	0.7	2.34	11.70
Block Design	1.28	0.9	1.0	3.18	15.90
Object Assembly	1.34	1.2	[0.93]	[3.47]	[17.35]
Coding	2.20	0.7	0.7	3.60	18.00
Picture Arrangement	0.93	1.9	[1.47]	[4.30]	[21.50]
Similarities	2.77	1.3	0.7	4.77	23.85
SUM[a]	11.63	7.9	6.1	25.63	
SUM[b]	11.63	7.9	5.3	24.83	

	Subtest sums	Full Scale IQ	Gain	Rate/year
WISC	100.00	100.00	–	–
WISC-R	111.63	107.63	7.63	0.311
WISC-III	119.53	113.00	5.47	0.322
WISC-IV[a]	125.63	117.63	4.63	0.363
WISC-IV[b]	124.83	116.83	3.83	0.300

[a]With values for OA and PA at those bracketed (see Flynn & Weiss, 2007).
[b]With values for OA and PA put at 0.80 for both (see Flynn & Weiss, 2007).

Trends on selected subtests

Similarities (1947–2002):	4.77 SS	= 1.59 SD	= 23.85 IQ
Digit Span (1972–2002):	0.20 SS	= 0.07 SD	= 1.00 IQ
Coding + Symbol Search (ave.) (1989–2002):	0.95 SS	= 0.32 SD	= 4.74 IQ

Sources:

Flynn (2000, Table 1); Psychological Corporation (2003, Table 5.8); Wechsler (1992, Table 6.8).

Notes:

(1) It is customary to score subtests on a scale in which the SD is 3, as opposed to IQ scores which are scaled with SD set at 15. To convert to IQ, just multiply subtest gains by 5, as was done to get the IQ gains in the last column.

(2) As to how the Full Scale IQs at the bottom of the table were derived:

1. The average member of the WISC sample (1947–1948) was set at 100.
2. The subtest gains by the WISC-R sample (1972) were summed and added to 100: $100 + 11.63 + 111.63$.
3. The appropriate conversion table was used to convert this sum into a Full Scale IQ score. The WISC-III table was chosen so that all samples would be scored against a common measure. That table equates 111.63 with an IQ of 107.63.
4. Thus the IQ gain from WISC to WISC-R was 7.63 IQ points.
5. Since the period between those two samples was 24.5 years, the rate of gain was 0.311 points per year (7.63 divided by $24.5 = 0.311$).
6. The subsequent gains are also calculated against the WISC sample, which is to say they are cumulative. By the time of the WISC-IV, closer to 2002 than 2001, you get a total IQ gain of somewhere between 16.83 and 17.63 IQ points over the whole period of 54.25 years. Taking the mid-point (17.23 points) gives an average rate of 0.318 points per year, with some minor variation (as the table shows) from one era to another.

Table 2 Effects on WISC subtests and Full Scale IQ from inbreeding. Outbred children (those with nil inbreeding) used to norm

	Nil	S&N (10%)	First cousins (6.25%)	Second cousins (1.56%)	WISC sample (36.00%)[a]
		SD = 3			
Coding	10	9.555	9.722	9.930	6.40
Arithmetic	10	9.495	9.684	9.921	9.54
Block Design	10	9.465	9.666	9.916	6.82
Picture Completion	10	9.410	9.631	9.908	7.66
Comprehension	10	9.395	9.622	9.906	7.80
Object Assembly	10	9.395	9.622	9.906	6.53
Information	10	9.170	9.481	9.870	9.57
Picture Arrangement	10	9.060	9.413	9.853	5.70
Similarities	10	9.005	9.378	9.845	5.23
Vocabulary	10	8.855	9.284	9.821	9.12
SUM SS	100	92.805	95.503	98.876	74.37
IQ (SD = 15)	100	94.963	96.851	99.211	81.21
IBD effect on SS		−7.195	−4.497	−1.124	−25.63[a]
IBD effect on IQ		−5.037	−3.149	−0.789	−18.79[a]

Sources:
Schull & Neel (1965, Table 12.19); Rushton (1995, Table 9.1).

[a] These values are hypothetical in the sense that they are those dictated by the hypothesis that IBD on the part of Americans in 1947 was responsible for their IQ deficits compared to Americans in 2002.

Notes:
(1) Conversion of sum of SS into IQs: (1) SS 90–100 = IQ 93–100, so within that range, 1.429 SS = 1 IQ; (2) SS 70–85 = IQ 78–89, so within that range, 1.364 SS = 1 IQ. Note that norming the 1947 children on 2002 gives a slightly different result than norming the 2002 children on 1947, as in Table 1. In the text, I have averaged out the two at 18 points.
(2) Mazes has been omitted as an eleventh subtest not normally used to calculate IQs.

Five tables have been promised. Table 1 simply details American IQ gains on the WISC.

Table 2 details my analysis of Schull and Neel's data on IBD (inbreeding depression) and requires a few explanatory comments.

In Table 2, "S&N" represent Schull and Neel's estimates of the SS deficit by subtest for each 10 percent of inbreeding. These allow us to calculate the magnitude of IBD (lower scores on the subtests) for the offspring of first cousins and the offspring of second cousins. The last column of Table 2 gives the much lower scores on each subtest for the children who were members of the WISC standardization sample of 1947–1948. These are derived from the fourth column of Table 1 by scoring them against the 2002 norms, which is to say they are the product of IQ gains over time.

The reader can see at a glance that the WISC children's score deficits are far greater than anything that could be explained by IBD, even if they were all assumed to be the offspring of first cousins. Their percentage of inbreeding would have to be 36 percent, as compared to first cousins at 6.25 percent! The conclusion: inbreeding depression cannot explain a significant portion of IQ gains over time.

Table 3 surveys all of the pairs of Wechsler and Stanford–Binet IQ tests that allow us to measure recent American IQ gains. When the same groups of subjects take both an older and a newer test, we get an estimate of IQ gains between the two years when the tests were normed. The average of twelve comparisons suggests that IQ gains have proceeded at a rate of 0.308 point per year. Note comparisons (1), (3), (9), and (12). They include the WAIS-III and tend to give both the largest and smallest rates of gain. If it is assumed that the WAIS-III inflates IQs by 2.34 points, discrepancies are much reduced. Deduct 2.34 from the gains in (1) and (3), where the WAIS-III is the earlier test, and add 2.34 to the gains in (9) and (12), where the WAIS-III is the later test. This gives rates of 0.526, 0.113, 0.308, and 0.273. Values larger or smaller than 2.34 increase discrepancies between the adjusted rates, so 2.34 points is the best estimate of how much the WAIS-III inflates IQs.

Appendix I

Table 3 Twelve estimates of recent IQ gains over time

Tests compared	Gains	Period (yrs)	Rate
(1) WAIS-III (1995) and SB-5 (2001)	+5.50	6	+0.917
(2) WAIS-R (1978) and SB-4 (1985)	+3.42	7	+0.489
(3) WAIS-III (1995) and WISC-IV (2001.75)	+3.10	6.75	+0.459
(4) WISC-III (1989) and SB-5 (2001)	+5.00	12	+0.417
(5) WISC-III (1989) and WISC-III/IV (2001.75)	+4.23	12.75	+0.332
(6) WISC-R (1972) and WISC-III (1989)	+5.30	17	+0.312
(7) WISC-R (1972) and SB-4 (1985)	+2.95	13	+0.227
(8) SB-4 (1985) and SB-5 (2001)	+2.77	16	+0.173
(9) WAIS-R (1978) and WAIS-III (1995)	+2.90	17	+0.171
(10) SB-LM (1972) and SB-4 (1985)	+2.16	13	+0.166
(11) WISC-R (1972) and WAIS-R (1978)	+0.90	6	+0.150
(12) WISC-III (1989) and WAIS-III (1995)	−0.70	6	−0.117
Average of all 12 comparisons			+0.308

Sources:
Flynn (2000, Table 1); Psychological Corporation (2003, Table 5.8);
Wechsler (1992, Table 6.8).

Test names and sources
(1) Wechsler Adult Intelligence Scale, 3rd edition (WAIS-III) and
    Stanford–Binet, 5th edition (SB-5): Roid (2003, Table 4.7)
(2) WAIS, revised and SB-4: Thorndike *et al.* (1986, Table 6.9)
(3) WAIS-III and Wechsler Intelligence Scale for Children, 4th edition
    (WISC-IV): Psychological Corporation (2003, Table 5.12)
(4) WISC, 3rd edition and SB-5: Roid (2003, Table 4.6)
(5) WISC-III and WISC-III/IV (see notes below): Flynn & Weiss (in press).
    The estimate given is the mid-point of the range of estimates for this
    pair of tests.
(6) WISC, revised and WISC-III: Flynn (1998c, Table 1)
(7) WISC-R and SB-4: Thorndike *et al.* (1986, Table 6.7)
(8) SB-4 and SB-5: Roid (2003, Table 4.1)
(9) WAIS-R and WAIS-III: Wechsler (1997, Table 4)
(10) Stanford–Binet LM and SB-4: Thorndike, Hagen, & Sattler (1986,
    Table 6.6)
(11) WISC-R and WAIS-R: Wechsler (1981, Table 18)
(12) WISC-III and WAIS-III: Wechsler (1997, Table 4.3)

Notes:

All dates assigned to tests refer to the date on which the test was normed. This is what is relevant not the publication date. Another date that scholars might like to have is that for the norming of the WISC: from 1947 to 1948.

Prior to the SB-5, the Stanford–Binet SD was set at 16 IQ points, rather than the usual 15 points. The above estimates are all based on scores adjusted to a common metric of SD = 15.

The alert reader will have noticed the peculiar label given to the test combination "WISC-III and WISC-III/IV." The WISC-IV dropped five of the ten subtests of the WISC-III and this renders the two non-comparable in terms of estimating the rate at which the WISC-III had become obsolete. Fortunately, the Psychological Corporation had collected special data (see source 9 above) that offered a solution. Flynn and Weiss (of the Psychological Corporation) used those data to simulate how the WISC-IV standardization sample would have performed on the unaltered WISC-III. They found that IQ scores would have been at least 1.33 points lower than the WISC-IV yielded. Thus the odd label WISC-III/IV, which refers to using a WISC-IV sample to assess norms for a test like the WISC-III.

Table 4 WISC IQ gains by IQ level: predicted gains vs. actual gain

WISC (1947.5) and WISC-R (1972)		WISC-R (1972) and WISC-III (1989)		WISC-III (1989) and WISC-III/IV (2001.75)	
IQ levels	P vs. A	IQ levels	P vs. A	IQ levels	P vs. A
125–140 = 118–133	7.35/6.67	128–140 = 121–133	5.10/6.60	145 = 140–145	3.825/3.83
115–125	7.35/	115–130	5.10/	130 = 126–131	3.825/3.83
105–115 = 97–107	7.35/8.30	110–115	5.10/	115 = 112–113	3.825/3.83
100–105	7.35/	100–110 = 94–104	5.10/6.02	100 = 96–98	3.825/4.33
90–100 = 81–91	7.35/8.52	90–100 = 86–94	5.10/4.01		
80–90 = 71–81	7.35/8.89	80–90 = 75–85	5.10/5.33	85 = 81–84	3.825/3.83
70–80 = 61–71	7.35/8.52	75–80 = 70–75	5.10/4.78	70 = 65–70	3.825/3.83
55–70 = 45–60	7.35/9.70	60–75 = 53–68	5.10/6.77	55 = 49–56	3.825/3.83
Weighted average	7.35/8.54	Weighted average	5.10/5.15	Average	3.825/3.90

Notes:

(1) Blanks indicate no data available.

(2) Numbers for each comparison (running from higher to lower IQs) are as follows: WISC and WISC-R 326, 415, 259, 170; WISC-R and WISC-III 652, 1055, 215, 108; WISC-III and WISC-III/IV 244 (only total for all subjects at all IQ levels is given).

(3) The data from the following sources have been analyzed and adapted. WISC and WISC-R: Flynn (1985, Table 2). WISC-R and WISC-III: Zimmerman & Woo-Sam (1997, Table 1) and Kanaya *et al.* (2003). WISC-III and WISC-III/IV: Psychological Corporation (2003, Table 5.9).

(4) WISC-R scores were adjusted to simulate scoring against the white members of the normative sample, thus allowing comparison with the WISC whose sample was whites only.

(5) Flynn and Weiss (2007) found that (at least) 1.33 points had to be deducted from WISC-IV IQs to equate them with WISC-III IQs; so that was added to the WISC-III and WISC-IV differences at all levels – to produce the "WISC-III and WISC-III/IV" differences.

Table 4 shows that at all IQ levels, WISC gains have been about 0.30 points per year during the period from 1947 to 2002. This is done by basing a predicted score difference on a rate of 0.30 points per year and comparing that to the actual difference.

Table 5 America from 1950 to 2000: rising percentage of employed civilians (16 years old and over) in professional, managerial, and technical occupations; effect on mean IQ and IQ threshold for that group of occupations

Year	Percentage	Mean IQ	IQ threshold
1950	17.03	114.50	103.82
1960	18.86	113.96	103.03
1970	21.42	113.27	102.00
1980	25.25	112.34	100.57
1990	29.37	111.43	99.16
2000	33.48	110.61	97.78

Sources:
US Bureau of the Census, 1975, Part 1, pp. 140–145, Series D 233–682; US Bureau of the Census, 1981, Labor Force, Employment, and Earnings, pp. 402–404, Table No. 675; US Bureau of the Census, 1990, Labor Force, Employment, and Earnings, pp. 395–397, Table No. 652; US Bureau of the Census, 2001, Labor Force, Employment, and Earnings, pp. 380–382, Table No. 593.

Notes:
(1) Working back from the year 2000, minor adjustments were made so that census job categories that were altered over time would match as closely as possible. Also earlier data were adjusted from 14 years old and over to 16 years old and over. The adjustments were minor, for example, the unadjusted figure for 1950 would be 17.35 percent.
(2) The calculations assume that the employed are a group with a mean IQ of 100. Probably, they are a bit elite in that those who are unemployed or outside the labor force tend to have below-average IQs. So, in reality, all the mean IQs and IQ thresholds would be a few points higher. For example, the values for 2000 are probably something like 112 and 100. But none of this affects the tendency over time of the mean IQ and IQ threshold to decrease.

Appendix I

(3) Example of calculations using year 2000:
1. Assume that the correlation between IQ and occupational status is perfect.
2. Since 33.48 percent are in PMT occupations, the bottom 66.52 percent of a normal curve is missing. That would push the mean IQ of this group to 1.0879 SDs above the mean.
3. However, the correlation between IQ and occupational status is not perfect. Putting it at 0.65, the IQ rise must be multiplied by that value.
4. So: $1.0879 \times 0.65 = 0.707$ SDs above the mean; 0.707×15 (SD of IQ) $= 10.61$; that $+100 = \mathbf{110.61}$ as estimated mean IQ.
5. Now to calculate the IQ threshold: a 0.707 rise in mean IQ would be obtained by eliminating the bottom 44.18% of a normal curve; the cutting line that eliminates the bottom 44.18% of a normal curve is 0.148 SDs below the mean; $0.148 \times 15 = 2.22$; that $-100 = \mathbf{97.78}$ as estimated IQ threshold.

Table 5 shows how much the percentage of Americans in high-status professions has grown over time and what this has done to lower the IQ threshold (needed to qualify) and the mean IQ of those professions.

Appendix II: Declaration in a capital case

There follows a sanitized version of a response to the report of a psychologist hired by the prosecution in a capital case. The detail is only slightly different from the John Doe case. I have repeated two figures from the body of this book to save the reader the trouble of referring back to them.

In a United States District Court unnamed

Declaration of James Robert Flynn, Ph.D.

I, James Robert Flynn, a competent adult, declare as follows:

1. I have been asked by post-conviction counsel for JD to respond to the Report of Dr. Prosecution. Except as otherwise indicated, all facts set forth in this declaration are based on my personal knowledge, research and analysis, which I conducted in accordance with the generally accepted norms of my profession.

2. For my work in this case, I am being compensated at a rate of $200 per hour. This represents a reduction of my usual rate based on the fact that the defendant is being represented on a *pro bono* basis. If called to testify in this case, I would provide the following testimony.

3. My credentials were established in my original declaration in this case.

4. I wish first to take up the central issue that Dr. P never addresses. The very meaning of an IQ of 70 is that you are

at about the 2nd percentile of your peers. By your peers, we mean a **representative** sample of **Americans** of your age cohort. Your age cohort is the people who were 13 years old the **same year** you were 13. I will discuss the three word(s) that are in bold.

5. When the defendant took the WISC-R at age 13 in 1991, he was being compared not to his peers but to the 13-year-olds of 1972 (when the test was normed). The 13-year-olds of those days were worse performers and so he ranked higher against them than against his peers. This gave him an inflated IQ of 71. Imagine that his school psychologist had given him the up-to-date version of the WISC, that is, the WISC-III, which was normed in 1989 and became available in 1991. A huge body of research shows that children who take both tests do 5 or 6 points worse (on average) on the newer test. And therefore, he would probably have got 65 or 66. Do we really want to make the death penalty a lottery dependent on what test a school psychologist happens to use?

6. Dr. P is disturbed that while the various combinations of tests show an average rate of obsolescence of 0.30 points per year, there is considerable variation from one combination of tests to another. Very well, since the defendant was tested on the WISC-R, let us confine ourselves to WISC data. Here there is very little variation on the rate of 0.30 points per year at any IQ level all the way from 1947 to 2002. As evidence, I have inserted Figure AII1, which is drawn from the WISC data in my original declaration.

7. Now even these highly consistent data only show that children **on average** got a bonus of almost 6 points if they took (as the defendant did) a version of the WISC nineteen years out of date. If he was dead average, his true IQ was 65 rather than 71. Perhaps he would actually have scored somewhere between 62 and 68. But one thing

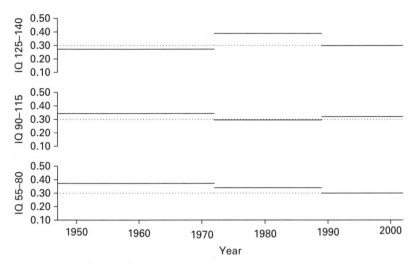

Figure AII1 Using the WISC to test whether the IQ gains of American children have been relatively uniform (about 0.30 points per year) between 1947 and 2002, and whether that has been true at all IQ levels. The three IQ levels I have chosen are 125–140 (high), 90–115 (average), and 55–80 (low). At each level, the broken line represents a gain of exactly 0.30 points per year. The solid lines show how little actual rates of gain have deviated from that value.

we do know is that 71 is too high and to leave it unadjusted is to give the worst possible estimate of his IQ. Imagine we found that someone had sneaked a group of children ten correct answers on the WISC. We then did studies that showed that the average child in the retardate range remembered six of them in the test room. Would we fail to adjust their IQ scores because we could not count on any individual being dead average? We would use the average of six because while there might be some individual variation, letting the scores stand would be absurd.

8. Dr. P notes that he has never seen a case in which a psychologist has altered an individual's score because of obsolescence. There is no reason why they should. They will administer the very latest test (unlike a school psychologist on a limited budget who has to use up her

backlog of the old edition). These days the tests are renormed every ten or fifteen years. The score is unlikely to be inflated by more than 3 points and that is unlikely to make him distrust his clinical judgment which is, after all, his main criterion of whether someone is MR. The Court is in a different position: 3 points may be the difference between life and death.

9. I cannot emphasize too strongly that failure to adjust scores is not suggested by prudence. No action is a decision and in these cases it lets a patently false score stand. A man in a clearing who sees a tiger charge at him can stand still because he does not know exactly how fast he can run to the nearest tree. Prudence does not recommend his choice.

10. We pass from the fact that a person's IQ should be scored against his peers to the fact that if he is an American, he should be scored against Americans. Dr. P notes studies that show that IQ gains have terminated (and therefore tests are not becoming obsolete) in Scandinavia. I think those studies are correct but they are no more relevant to what is going on in America than studies that show that, in rural Kenya, people are gaining at twice the rate we find in America (Daley et al., 2003). Dr. Weiss of the Psychological Corporation (publishers of the Wechsler tests) has co-authored a paper with me that shows gains continuing in America at the same old rate. My original declaration refers to it plus a wealth of evidence that points in the same direction.

11. We pass on to the fact that you must be scored against a sample of your peers that is representative. It is certain test combinations, those in which at least one test is designed for adults, which show the greatest variation. This is because it is much harder to get a representative sample of American adults than of schoolchildren. With the latter,

so long as you pick a group of schools stratified for SES, region, and so forth, the children are "trapped" there waiting to be tested. There is no similar institution that captures a representative sample of American adults. They are dispersed in their various homes and places of work.

12. Dr. P cites my compliment to the architects of the WAIS-III for their efforts to get a good sample of low-IQ subjects. I stand by that compliment but they cannot do the impossible. The overall norms of an adult test are set by the total sample and they just had bad luck and got a sample that was slightly substandard. Comparisons involving the WAIS-III stand out like a sore thumb. In every test pair in which it was the earlier test, it inflates the rate of gain far above 0.30 because it makes the earlier test scores seem too high. In every test pair in which it was the later test, it reduces the rate of gain to practically nil because, once again, it makes the later test scores look too high. As evidence, I have inserted Figure AII2. As I said in my original declaration, the assumption that brings the WAIS-III closest to other IQ tests is that it inflates IQs by 2.34 points.

13. It remains only to comment on a few of Dr. P's remaining points:

    (1) On page 4, he says that the Psychological Corporation stands behind the quality of the WAIS-III normative sample. No test publisher is going to indict their own sample, particularly when they did such a good job of trying to get a representative sample. I cannot see a thing wrong with their procedures. But once again, on an adult sample, you can have plain bad luck.

    (2) On page 5, I have dealt with his citation of the Scandinavian data. He cites Wicherts *et al.* (2004) concerning the fact that IQ gains over time are eccentric given the various cognitive skills measured by the

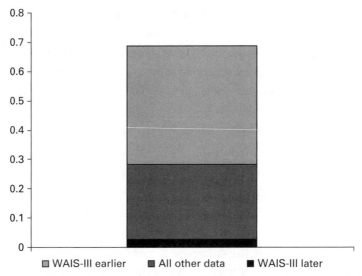

Figure AII2 Note the inflated rate of gain (.688) when the WAIS-III is the earlier test and the virtually nil rate (.027) when the WAIS-III is the later test in a combination.

subtests. They are indeed, but here we are concerned with Full Scale IQ and no scholar, including Wicherts, prefers obsolete norms to current ones.

(3) Page 2 of the four pages of correspondence between Dr. P and test publishers makes interesting reading. I quote the email of June 23, 2006: "We will get a hold of it to see how Flynn got the 2.34 point increase. I am not surprised though. It has been eight years since the WAIS-III was published, and Flynn's previous publication would indicate that his number is about right." As Dr. P notes, they were confused about the question at issue in that they thought obsolescence was being discussed. However, note how they do endorse a rate of .30 points a year as "about right" for obsolescence: 8 years × .30 = 2.4 points, making 2.34 points seem about right.

14. I have no expectation that psychologists in a normal clinical setting, or a test publisher advising psychologists in such settings, are going to adjust obsolete IQ scores. But the Court is not in that position. It must decide either to make the death penalty less of a lottery; or to refrain from doing so, simply because it is not sure just how much it is remedying the situation.

I declare under penalty of perjury that the forgoing is true and correct.

James Robert Flynn, Ph.D.

References

American Association on Mental Retardation (2002). *Mental retardation: Definition, classification, and systems of support*, 10th edn. Washington, DC: American Association on Mental Retardation.

Andel, R., Crowe, M., Pedersen, N. L., Mortimer, J., Crimmins, E., & Gatz, M. (2005). Complexity of work and risk of Alzheimer's disease: A population-based study of Swedish twins. *Journals of Gerontology Series B: Psychological Sciences and Social Science*, 60: 251–258.

Andrich, D., & Styles, I. (1994). Psychometric evidence of intellectual growth spurts in early adolecence. *Journal of Early Adolescence*, 14: 328–344.

Aristotle. The citations in the text will guide the reader to the source. All editions of Aristotle, no matter what the publisher and date, have the same chapter and page numbers in the margins and those are what are cited herein.

Atkins v. *Virginia*, 536 U.S. 304, 122 S.CT 2242 (2002).

Black v. *State*, No. M2004-01345-CCA-R3-PD, 2005 Tenn. Crim. App. LEXIS 1129 (Tenn. 2005).

Blair, C. (2006). How similar are fluid cognition and general intelligence? A developmental neuroscience perspective on fluid cognition as an aspect of human cognitive ability. *Behavioral and Brain Sciences*, 29: 109–160.

Blair, C., Gamson, D., Thorne, S., & Baker, D. (2005). Rising mean IQ: Cognitive demand of mathematics education for young children, population exposure to formal schooling, and the neurology of the prefrontal cortex. *Intelligence*, 33: 93–106.

Blanchflower, D. G., Oswald, A. J., & Warr, P. B. (1993). Well-being over time in Britain and the USA. Paper presented at the Economics of Happiness Conference, London School of Economics.

Bouvier, U. (1969). *Evolution des côtes à quelques tests* [Evolution of scores from several tests]. Brussels: Belgian Armed Forces, Center for Research Into Human Traits.

Bowling v. *Commonwealth*, 163 S.W.3d 361 (Ky. 2005).

Callaway, E. (1975). *Brain electrical potentials and individual psychological differences.* New York: Grune & Statton.

Cannell, J. J. (1988). Nationally normed elementary achievement testing in America's public schools: How all fifty states are above the national average. Unpublished paper, Friends for Education.

Case, R., Demetriou, A., Platsidou, M., & Katz, S. (2001). Integrating concepts and tests of intelligence from the differential and developmental traditions. *Intelligence*, 29: 307–336.

Clarke, A. D. (1973). The prevention of subcultural subnormality: Problems and prospects. *British Journal of Subnormality*, 19: 7–20.

Clarke, S. C. T., Nyberg, V., & Worth, W. H. (1978). *Technical report on Edmonton Grade III achievement: 1956–1977 comparisons.* Edmonton, Canada: University of Alberta.

Cohen, G. D. (2005). *The mature mind: The positive power of the aging brain.* New York: Basic Books.

Colom, R., Flores-Mendoza, C. E., & Abad, F. J. (in press). Generational changes on the Draw-a-Man test: A comparison of Brazilian urban and rural children tested in 1930, 2002, and 2004.

Colom, R., Lluis Font, J. M., & Andres-Pueyo, A. (2005). The generational intelligence gains are caused by decreasing variance in the lower half of the distribution: Supporting evidence for the nutrition hypothesis. *Intelligence*, 33: 83–92.

Daley, T. C., Whaley, S. E., Sigman, M. D., Espinosa, M. P., & Neumann, C. (2003). IQ on the rise: The Flynn effect in rural Kenyan children. *Psychological Science*, 14: 215–219.

References

Deary, I. J. (2001). *Intelligence: A very short introduction*. Oxford: Oxford. University Press.

Deary, I. J., & Crawford, J. R. (1998). A triarchic theory of Jensenism: Persistent, conservative reductionism. *Intelligence*, 26: 273–282.

Dickens, W. T. (2004). Extending and testing the reciprocal effects model. Brookings proposal to the National Institute on Ageing.

Dickens, W. T., & Flynn, J. R. (2001a). Great leap forward: A new theory of intelligence. *New Scientist*, April 21, 44–47.

(2001b). Heritability estimates versus large environmental effects: The IQ paradox resolved. *Psychological Review*, 108: 346–369.

(2006). Black Americans reduce the racial IQ gap: Evidence from standardization samples. *Psychological Science*, 17: 913–920.

Duckworth, A. L., & Seligman, M. E. P. (2005). Self-discipline outdoes IQ in predicting academic performance. *Psychological Science*, 16: 939–944.

Easterlin, R. (1974). Does economic growth improve the human lot? Some empirical evidence. In P. A. David & M. W. Reder (eds.), *Nations and households in economic growth: Essays in honor of Moses Abramovitz*. New York and London: Academic Press.

(1995). Will raising the incomes of all increase the happiness of all? *Journal of Economic Behaviour and Organization*, 27: 35–48.

Emanuelsson, I., Reuterberg, S.-E., & Svensson, A. (1993). Changing differences in intelligence? Comparisons between groups of thirteen-year-olds tested from 1960 to 1990. *Scandinavian Journal of Educational Research*, 37: 259–277.

Endler, L. C., & Bond, T. G. (in press). Tracking development with the Rasch Model: Empirical evidence of growth and heterogeneity. In X. Liu & W. Boone (eds.), *Applications of Rasch measurement in science education*. Maple Grove, MN: JAM Press.

Ex parte Murphy, No. WR-38, 198-03, 2006 Tex. Crim., App. (Tex., Jan. 18, 2006).

Faulks, S. (2006). *Human traces*. London: Vintage Books.

Flieller, A. (1999). Comparison of the development of formal thought in adolescent cohorts aged 10 to 15 years (1967–1996 and 1972–1993). *Developmental Psychology*, 35: 1048–1058.

Flieller, A., Saintigny, N., & Schaeffer, R. (1986). L'évolution du niveau intellectuel des enfants de 8 ans sur une période de 40 ans, 1944–1984 [The evolution of the intellectual level of 8-year-old children over a period of 40 years, 1944–1984]. *L'orientation scolaire et professionelle*, 15: 61–83.

Flynn, J. R. (1984a). IQ gains and the Binet decrements. *Journal of Educational Measurement*, 21: 283–290.

(1984b). The mean IQ of Americans: Massive gains 1932 to 1978. *Psychological Bulletin*, 95: 29–51.

(1985). Wechsler intelligence tests: Do we really have a criterion of mental retardation? *American Journal of Mental Deficiency*, 90: 236–244.

(1987). Massive IQ gains in 14 nations: What IQ tests really measure. *Psychological Bulletin*, 101: 171–191.

(1991a). *Asian Americans: Achievement beyond IQ*. Hillsdale, NJ: Erlbaum.

(1991b). Reaction times show that both Chinese and British children are more intelligent than one another. *Perceptual and Motor Skills*, 72: 544–546.

(1993a). Derrida: What does he believe? *Political Theory Newsletter*, 5: 180–181.

(1993b). Skodak and Skeels: The inflated mother-child IQ gap. *Intelligence*, 17: 557–561.

(1998a). IQ gains over time: Toward finding the causes. In U. Neisser (ed.), *The rising curve: Long-term gains in IQ and related measures* (pp. 25–66). Washington, DC: American Psychological Association.

(1998b). Israeli military IQ tests: Gender differences small; IQ gains large. *Journal of Biosocial Science*, 30: 541–553.

(1998c). WAIS-III and WISC-III: IQ gains in the United States from 1972 to 1995; how to compensate for obsolete norms. *Perceptual and Motor Skills*, 86: 1231–1239.

(2000a). *How to defend humane ideals: Substitutes for objectivity.* Lincoln, NB: University of Nebraska Press.

(2000b). IQ gains, WISC subtests, and fluid *g*: *g* theory and the relevance of Spearman's hypothesis to race (followed by Discussion). In G. R. Bock, J. A. Goode, & K. Webb (eds.), *The nature of intelligence* (pp. 202–227). Novartis Foundation Symposium 233. New York: Wiley.

(2000c). The hidden history of IQ and special education: Can the problems be solved? *Psychology, Public Policy, and Law,* 6: 191–198.

(2006a). Efeito Flynn: Repensando a inteligência e seus efeitos [The Flynn effect: Rethinking intelligence and what affects it]. In C. Flores-Mendoza & R. Colom (eds.), *Introdução à psicologia das diferenças individuais* (pp. 387–411). [Introduction to the psychology of individual differences]. Porto Alegre, Brazil: ArtMed. (English trans: jim.flynn@stonebow.otago.ac.nz)

(2006b). Tethering the elephant: Capital cases, IQ, and the Flynn effect. *Psychology, Public Policy, and Law,* 12: 170–178.

(in press). The America who would be king. In David MacDonald & Robert Patman (eds.), *Ethics of foreign policy.* Aldershot, UK: Ashgate Press.

(under review). Has Michael Shayer found the Holy Grail? Teaching mathematics, Piagetian skills, and the WISC subtests.

Flynn, J. R., & Dickens, W. T. (under review). Black men and women: The marriage market of perpetual war.

Flynn, J. R., & Rossi-Casé, L. (under review). Beyond skulls and genes: Raven's and gender equality; also new massive IQ gains.

Flynn, J. R., & Weiss, L. G. (2007). American IQ gains from 1932 to 2002: The WISC subtests and educational progress. *International Journal of Testing,* 7: 1–16.

Folger, J. K., & Nam, C. B. (1967). *Education of the American population* (A 1960 Census Monograph). Washington, DC: US Department of Commerce.

French, J. L. (2001). *Pictorial test of intelligence*, 2nd edn. Austin, TX: PRO-ED.

Frey, B., & Stutzer, A. (1999). Happiness, economics, and institutions. Unpublished paper, University of Zurich.

Frumkin, I. B. (Fall 2003). *Mental retardation: A primer to cope with expert testimony.* Access: http://www.nlada.org/DMS/ Documents 1066919805.15/Mental%20Retardation.pdf See p. 3 (as of Jan. 6, 2006).

Furman v. Georgia, 408 U.S. 238 (1972).

Garber, H. L. (1988). *The Milwaukee Project: Preventing mental retardation in children at risk.* Washington, DC: American Association on Mental Retardation.

Goleman, D. P. (1995). *Emotional intelligence.* New York: Bantam. (1998). *Working with emotional intelligence.* New York: Bantam.

Gottfredson, L. S. (2001). Book review: "Practical intelligence in everyday life." *Intelligence*, 29: 363–365.

Green, S., & Bavelier, D. (2003). Action video game modifies visual selective attention. *Nature*, 423: 534–537.

Greenfield, P. (1998). The cultural evolution of IQ. In U. Neisser (ed.), *The rising curve: Long-term gains in IQ and related measures* (pp. 81–123). Washington, DC: American Psychological Association.

Hallpike, C. R. (1979). *The foundations of primitive thought.* Oxford: Clarendon Press.

Hare, R. M. (1963). *Freedom and reason.* London: Oxford University Press.

Heckman, J. J., & Rubenstein, Y. (2001). The importance of non-cognitive skills: Lessons from the GED testing program. *American Economic Review*, 91: 145–149.

Heckman, J. J., Stixrud, J., & Urzua, S. (2006). The effects of cognitive and non-cognitive abilities on labor market outcomes and social behavior. *Journal of Labor Economics*, 24: 411–482.

Herrnstein, R. J., & Murray, C. (1994). *The bell curve: Intelligence and class in American life.* New York: Free Press.

Hoosain, R. (1991). *Psycholinguistic implications for linguistic relativity: A case study of Chinese.* Hillsdale, NJ: Erlbaum.

References

Howard, R. W. (1999). Preliminary real-world evidence that average intelligence really is rising. *Intelligence*, 27: 235–250.

In re Hicks, 375 F.3d 1237 (11th Cir. 2004).

Jensen, A. R. (1972). *Genetics and education*. London: Methuen.

(1973a). *Educability and group differences*. New York: Harper & Row.

(1973b). *Educational differences*. London: Methuen.

(1979). The nature of intelligence and its relation to learning. *Journal of Research and Development in Education*, 12: 79–85.

(1980). *Bias in mental testing*. London: Methuen.

(1981). *Straight talk about mental tests*. New York: Free Press.

(1983). Effects of inbreeding on mental-ability factors. *Personality and Individual Differences*, 4: 71–87.

(1998). *The g factor: The science of mental ability*. Westport, CT: Praeger.

Jensen, A. R., & Whang, P. A. (1994). Speed of accessing arithmetic facts in long term memory: A comparison of Chinese American and Anglo-American children. *Contemporary Educational Psychology*, 19: 1–12.

Johnson, S. (2005). *Everything bad is good for you: How today's popular culture is actually making us smarter*. New York: Rimerhead Books.

Kanaya, T., Scullin, M. H., & Ceci, S. J. (2003). The Flynn effect and US policies: The impact of rising IQ scores on American society via mental retardation diagnoses. *American Psychologist* 58: 778–790.

Kawashima, H., & Matsuyama, T. (2005). Multiphase learning for an interval based hybrid dynamical system. *IEICE Transactions Fundamentals*, E88-A: 3022–3035.

Kelley, R., & Caplan, J. (1993). How Bell Labs creates star performers. *Harvard Business Review*, 71: 128–139.

Krugman, P. (1994). *Peddling poverty: Economic sense and nonsense in the age of diminished expectations*. New York: W. W. Norton.

Leong, F. T. L., Hartung, P. J., Goh, D., & Gaylor, M. (2001). Appraising birth order in career assessment: Linkages to Holland's and Super's models. *Journal of Career Assessment*, 9: 25–39.

Lewontin, R. C. (1976a). Further remarks on race and the genetics of intelligence. In N. J. Block & G. Dworkin (eds.), *The IQ controversy* (pp. 107–112). New York: Pantheon Books.

(1976b). Race and intelligence. In N. J. Block & G. Dworkin (eds.), *The IQ controversy* (pp. 78–92). New York: Pantheon Books.

Luria, A. R. (1976). *Cognitive development: Its cultural and social foundations*. Cambridge MA: Harvard University Press.

Lynn, R. (1987). Japan: Land of the rising IQ. A reply to Flynn. *Bulletin of the British Psychological Society*, 40: 464–468.

(1989). Positive correlation between height, head size and IQ: A nutrition theory of the secular increases in intelligence. *British Journal of Educational Psychology*, 59: 372–377.

(1996a). *Dysgenics: Genetic deterioration in modern populations*. Westport, CT: Praeger.

(1996b). Racial and ethnic differences in intelligence in the United States on the Differential Ability Scale. *Personality and Individual Differences*, 20: 271–273.

(in press). The intelligence of East Asians: A thirty year controversy and its resolution. *The Mankind Quarterly*.

Lynn, R., Chan, J. W., & Eysenck, H. J. (1991). Reaction times and intelligence in Chinese and British children. *Perceptual and Motor Skills*, 72: 443–452.

Lynn, R., & Vanhanen, T. (2002). *IQ and the wealth of nations*. Westport, CT: Praeger.

Lynn, R., & Van Court, M. (2004). New evidence of dysgenic fertility for intelligence in the United States. *Intelligence*, 32: 193–201.

Mackintosh, N. J. (2006). Comments on Flynn, "Beyond the Flynn effect." At the symposium sponsored by Cambridge Assessment, Trinity College, Cambridge, 15 December 2006.

Maguire, E. A., Gadian, D. G., Johnsrude, I. S., Good, C. D., Ashburner, J., Frackowiak, R. S. J., & Frith, C. D. (2000). Navigation-related structural change in the hippocampi of taxi drivers. *Proceedings of the National Academy of Sciences*, 97: 4398–4403.

Martorell, R. (1998). Nutrition and the worldwide rise in IQ scores. In U. Neisser (ed.), *The rising curve: Long-term gains in IQ and related measures* (pp. 183–206). Washington, DC: American Psychological Association.

McKenzie, D. J. (2006). Disentangling age, cohort and time effects in the additive model. *Oxford Bulletin of Economics and Statistics*, 68: 473–495.

Meisenberg, G., Lawless, E., Lambert, E., & Newton, A. (2005). The Flynn effect in the Caribbean: Generational change in test performance in Dominica. *Mankind Quarterly*, 46: 29–70.

Melton, L. (2005). Use it, don't lose it. *New Scientist*, December 17: 32–35.

Mosler, D., & Catley, B. (1998). *America and Americans in Australia.* Westport, CT: Praeger.

Mussen, P. H., Conger, J. J., & Kagan, J. (1974). *Child development and personality*, 4th edn. New York: Harper & Row.

Must, O., Must, A., & Raudik, V. (2003). The secular rise in IQs: In Estonia, the Flynn effect is not a Jensen effect. *Intelligence*, 31: 461–471.

Myers v. State, 278 P. 1106 (Okla. 2005).

Nettelbeck, T. (1998). Jensen's chronometric research: Neither simple nor sufficient but a good place to start. *Intelligence*, 26: 233–241.

Nevo, B. S. (2002). Humane Egalitarian Democratic Values Questionnaire (HED-VQ-1): Results of a pilot study. Unpublished manuscript. Available from jim.flynn@stonebow.otago.ac.nz

Nunn, J. (1999). *John Nunn's chess puzzle book.* London: Gambit.

Offer, A. (2006). *The challenge of affluence: Self-control and well-being in the United Sates and Britain since 1950.* New York: Oxford University Press.

Olmstead, F. L. (1969). *The cotton kingdom.* New York: Modern Library.

Oswald, A. J. (1997). Happiness and economic performance. *The Economic Journal*, 107: 1815–1831.

People v. *Superior Court (Vidal)*, 129 Cal. App. 4th 434, 28 Cal Rptr. 3d 529 (5th Ct. App. 2005), *vacated and later proceedings at People v. S.C.*, 2005 Cal. LEXIS 13290 (Cal., Nov. 17, 2005).

Psychological Corporation (2003). *The WISC-IV technical manual.* San Antonio, TX: The Psychological Corporation.

Raven, J. (2000). *Raven manual research supplement 3: American norms; neuropsychological applications.* Oxford: Oxford Psychologists Press.

Raven, J., Raven, J. C., & Court, J. H. (1993). *Manual for Raven's Progressive Matrices and Vocabulary Scales* (section 1). Oxford: Oxford Psychologists Press.

Reid, N., & Gilmore, A. (1988). The Raven's Standard Progressive Matrices in New Zealand. Paper given at Australian Council for Educational Research (ACER) Seminar on Intelligence, Melbourne, Australia.

Reuters (1995). Children working have higher IQs, study shows. *Otago Daily Times*, June 14, 1995, p. 34.

Roid, G. H. (2003). *Stanford–Binet Intelligence Scales,* 5th edn. *Technical manual.* Itasca, IL: Riverside.

Rosenau, J. N., & Fagan, W. M. (1997). A new dynamism in world politics: Increasingly skilled individuals? *International Studies Quarterly*, 41: 655–686.

Ross, P. E. (2006). The expert mind. *Scientific American*, 295 (2): 64–71.

Rushton, J. P. (1995). *Race, evolution and behavior: A life history perspective.* New Brunswick, NJ: Transaction Publishers.
  (1997). Cranial size and IQ in Asian Americans from birth to seven. *Intelligence*, 25: 7–20.

Rutter, J. M. (2000). Comments in discussion on James R. Flynn. In G. R. Bock & J. Goode (eds.), *The nature of intelligence* (pp. 222–223). Novartis Foundation Symposium 233. New York: Wiley.

Salthouse, T. A. (2006). Mental exercise and mental aging: Evaluating the validity of the "Use it or lose it" hypothesis. *Perspectives on Psychological Science*, 1: 68–87.

Schaie, K. W., & Hertzog, C. (1983). Fourteen-year cohort sequential analysis of adult intellectual development. *Developmental Psychology*, 19: 531–543.

Schneider, D. (2006). Smart as we can get? *American Scientist*, 94: 311–312.

Schooler, C. (1998). Environmental complexity and the Flynn effect. In U. Neisser (ed.), *The rising curve: Long-term gains in IQ and related measures* (pp. 67–79). Washington, DC: American Psychological Association.

Schull, W. J., & Neel, J. V. (1965). *The effects of inbreeding on Japanese children*. New York: Harper & Row.

Scullin, M. H. (in press). Large state-level fluctuations in mental retardation classifications related to introduction of renormed intelligence test. *American Journal on Mental Retardation*.

Shayer, M., & Adhami, M. (2003). Realising the cognitive potential of children 5–7 with a mathematical focus. *International Journal of Educational Research*, 39: 743–775.

(in press). Fostering cognitive development through the context of mathematics: Results of the CAME Project. *Educational Studies in Mathematics*.

Shayer, M., Ginsburg, D., & Coe, R. (in press). 30 years on – an anti-"Flynn effect"? The Piagetian test *Volume & Heaviness* norms 1975–2003. *British Journal for Educational Psychology*.

Shayer, M., Küchemann, D. E., & Wylam, H. (1976). The distribution of Piagetian stages of thinking in British middle and secondary school children. *British Journal of Educational Psychology*, 46: 164–173.

Skodak, M. D., & Skeels, H. M. (1949). A final follow-up study of one hundred adopted children. *Journal of Genetic Psychology*, 75: 85–125.

Springer, M. (2006). Champ chimp. *Scientific American Mind*, 17 (4): 12–14.

State v. *Burke*, 2005 Ohio 7020 (2005).

State v. *Murphy*, 2005 Ohio 423 (2005).

Sternberg, R. J. (1988). *The triarchic mind: A new theory of human intelligence*. New York: Penguin.

(1999). Review of "Working with emotional intelligence." *Personnel Psychology*, 52: 780–781.

(2006). The Rainbow Project: Enhancing the SAT through assessments of analytic, practical, and creative skills. *Intelligence*, 34: 321–350.

Sternberg, R. J., Forsythe, G. B., Hedlund, J., Horvath, J. A., Wagner, R. K., Williams, W. M., Snook, S. A., & Grigorenko, E. L. (2000). *Practical intelligence in everyday life*. New York: Cambridge University Press.

Storfer, M. D. (1990). *Intelligence and giftedness: The contributions of heredity and early environment*. San Francisco: Jossey-Bass.

Styles, I. (in press). Linking psychometric and cognitive-developmental frameworks for thinking about intellectual functioning. In J. Raven (ed.), *Contributions to psychological and psychometric theory arising from studies with Raven's Progressive Matrices and Vocabulary Scales*.

Sundet, J. M., Barlaug, D. G., & Torjussen, T. M. (2004). The end of the Flynn effect? A study of secular trends in mean intelligence test scores of Norwegian conscripts during half a century. *Intelligence*, 32: 349–362.

Tawney, R. H. (1931). *Equality*. London: Allen & Unwin.

Teasdale, T. W., & Owen, D. R. (1989). Continued secular increases in intelligence and a stable prevalence of high intelligence levels. *Intelligence*, 13: 255–262.

(2000). Forty-year secular trends in cognitive abilities. *Intelligence*, 28: 115–120.

Thorndike, E. L. (1920). Intelligence and its uses. *Harper's Magazine*, 140: 227–235.

Thorndike, R. L., Hagen, E. P., & Sattler, J. M. (1986). *The Stanford–Binet Intelligence Scale*, 4th edn. *Technical manual*. Chicago: Riverside Publishing Company.

Toulmin, S. E. (1960). *Reason in ethics*, 1st paperback edn. Cambridge: Cambridge University Press.

References

Trowbridge, B. (April 2003). *US Supreme Court finds execution of the mentally retarded "cruel and unusual"; you have to pass a test before you can be put to death?* Access: http://www.trowbridgefoundation.org/docs/ execution.htm. See pp. 7–8 (as of Jan. 6, 2006).

Tuddenham, R. D. (1948). Soldier intelligence in World Wars I and II. *American Psychologist*, 3: 54–56.

US Bureau of the Census (1975). *Historical statistics of the United States, colonial times to 1970* (1975 bicentennial edn).

US Bureau of the Census (1981). *Statistical abstract of the United States.*

US Bureau of the Census (1990). *Statistical abstract of the United States.*

US Bureau of the Census (2001). *Statistical abstract of the United States.*

US Department of Education. Institute of Education Sciences. National Center for Educational Statistics (2003). *The nation's report card: Reading 2002*, NCES 2003-521, by W. S. Grigg, M. C. Daane, Y. Jin, and J. R. Campbell. Washington, DC.

US Department of Education. Office of Educational Research and Improvement. National Center for Educational Statistics (2000). *NAEP 1996 trends in academic progress*, NCES 97-985r, by J. R. Campbell, K. E. Voelkl, and P. L. Donahue. Washington, DC.

US Department of Education. Office of Educational Research and Improvement. National Center for Educational Statistics (2001). *The nation's report card: Mathematics 2000*, NCES 2001-517, by J. S. Braswell, A. D. Lutkus, W. S. Grigg, S. L. Santapau, B. Tay-Lim, and M. Johnson. Washington, DC.

Veenhoven, Ruut (1993). *Happiness in nations: Subjective appreciation of life in 56 nations*. Rotterdam: Erasmus University Risbo.

Vernon, P. E. (1982). *The abilities and achievements of orientals in North America*. New York: Academic Press.

References

Vineland (2006). Pre-publication data from the Vineland-II manual courtesy of S. Sparrow, Ph.D., Professor Emerita and Senior Research Scientist, Yale Child Study Center.

Vroon, P. A. (1984). Raven's score distribution of Dutch draftees. Personal communication, November 5.

Walker v. *True*, 399 F.3d 315 (4th Cir. 2005), *after remand*, 401 F.3d 574 (4th Cir. 2005).

Walton v. *Johnson*, 407 F.3d 285, 295–97 (4th Cir. 2005).

Wechsler, D. (1955). *Wechsler Adult Intelligence Scale: Manual*. New York: The Psychological Corporation.

(1974). *Wechsler Intelligence Scale for Children – Revised*. New York: The Psychological Corporation.

(1981). *Wechsler Adult Intelligence Scale – Revised: Manual*. New York: The Psychological Corporation.

(1992). *Wechsler Intelligence Scale for Children*, 3rd edn. *Manual* (Australian Adaptation). San Antonio, TX: The Psychological Corporation.

(1997). *Wechsler Adult Intelligence Scale*, 3rd edn. *Manual*. San Antonio, TX: The Psychological Corporation.

Weyl, N. (1966). *The creative elite in America*. Washington, DC: Public Affairs Press.

(1969). Some comparative performance indexes of American ethnic minorities. *Mankind Quarterly*, 9: 106–119.

Wicherts, J. M., Dolan, C. V., Hessen, D. J., Oosterveld, P., van Baal, G. C. M., Boomsma, D. I., & Span M. M. (2004). Are intelligence tests measurement invariant over time? Investigating the Flynn effect. *Intelligence*, 32: 509–538.

Zimmerman, I. L., & Woo-Sam, J. M. (1997). Review of the criterion-related validity of the WISC-III: The first five years. *Perceptual and Motor Skills*, 85: 531–546.

Subject index

Subject index

Subject index

Name index

Abad, F. J. 170
Adhami, M. 17, 31
American Association on Mental
  Retardation (AAMR) 125
Andel, R. 64
Andres-Pueyo, A. 104
Andrich, D. 33
Archimedes 160
Aristotle 48, 51, 77, 79, 83, 143, 160–161,
  166, 170
Augustine, Saint 157

Baker, D. 16
Barlaug, D. G. 104, 105
Bavelier, D. 72
Benedict, Ruth 150
Berkeley, Bishop 163
Blair, Clancy 16, 60, 66, 67, 68, 76, 82
Blanchflower, D. G. 165
Bond, T. G. 30, 31, 80
Bouvier, U. 104
Bush, George (Sn) 167
Bush, George (Jr) 167
Butler, Bishop Joseph 170

Callaway, E. 73
Cannell, J. J. 114
Caplan, J. 77
Case, R. 35
Catley, B. 102
Ceci, Steve 82, 128
Chan, J. W. 74
Churchill, Winston 167
Clarke, A. D. 124
Clarke, S. C. T. 104

Coe, R. 17
Cohen, G. D. 64, 68, 76
Colom, Roberto xi, 82, 104, 170
Conger, J. J. 124
Court, J. H. 23
Crawford, J. R. 71
Cromwell, Oliver 171

Daley, D. C. 144, 192
Deary, Ian 71, 72, 82
Demetriou, A. 35
Derrida, J. 151–152
Descartes, René 52
Dickens, William T. 38, 60, 64, 82, 83,
  92, 93, 96, 97, 98, 123, 142, 148
Duckworth, A. L. 77, 78, 168

Easterlin, R. 165, 166
Educational Testing Service (ETS) 115
Einstein, Albert 52, 160
Emanuelsson, I. 104
Endler, L. C. 30
Eysenck, Hans 74

Fagan, W. M. 162
Faulks, Sebastian vi
Flieller, A. 31, 108
Flores-Mendoza, C. E. xi, 170
Flynn, James R. xi, 4, 8, 14, 17, 32, 35, 60,
  63, 64, 74, 83, 89–92, 94, 97, 98, 103,
  104, 107, 116, 118, 120, 123, 127, 130,
  131, 133, 135, 137, 142, 143, 145, 148,
  150, 158, 160, 167, 168, 181, 184,
  185, 186
Folger, J. K. 32

Name index

Rabin, I. 167
Raudic, V. 104
Raven, John 23, 33, 82
Raven, J. C. 23
Reed, Congressman 167
Reid, N. 125
Reuterberg, S.-E. 104
Reuters 114
Robeson, Paul 157
Roid, G. H. 184
Rosenau, J. N. 162
Ross, P. E. 88
Rossi-Casé, L. 8, 104
Rubenstein, Y. 77
Rushton, J. P. 97, 101, 121, 182
Russell, Bertram 150
Rutter, Sir Michael 103

Saintigny, N. 108
Salthouse, T. A. 65
Sattler, J. M. 184
Schaeffer, R. 108
Schaie, K. W. 96
Schneider, D. 143
Schooler, Carmi 43, 100
Schull, W. J. 101–102, 182
Scullin, M. H. 128, 129
Seligman, M. E. P. 77, 78, 168
Sharon, A. 167
Shayer, Michael 17, 31, 82
Skeels, H. M. 124
Skodak, M. D. 124
Smith, Adam 147
Sowell, Thomas 157
Springer, M. 72
Sternberg, R. J. 54, 78–80, 82
Stixrud, J. 78
Storfer, M. D. 103
Stutzer, A. 166

Stewart, W. (Justice) 111, 131
Styles, I. 33
Sumner, William Graham 148, 152
Sundet, J. M. 104, 105
Svensson, A. 104

Tawney, R. N. 141
Teasdale, T. W. 104
Thorndike, E. L. 77, 184
Thorne, S. 16
Torjussen, T. M. 104, 105
Toulmin, S. E. 1
Trowbridge, B. 133
Tuddenham, R. D. 2, 23, 108

Urzua, S. 78
US Bureau of the Census 187
US Department of Education 20, 21

Van Court, M. 101
Vanhanen, T. 144
Veenhoven, Ruut 165
Vernon, P. E. 116–117
Vineland 126
Vroon, P. A. 2, 104

Warr, P. D. 165
Wechsler, D. 27, 28, 104, 130, 181, 184
Weiss, Lawrence G. xi, 143, 184, 185, 186, 192
Weyl, N. 115
Whang, P. A. 121
Wicherts, J. M. 18, 193
Williams, Wendy 82
Woo-Sam, J. M. 186
Worth, W. H. 104
Wylam, H. 31

Zimmerman, I. L. 186